IMPLEMENTING MANAGEMENT INNOVATIONS
Lessons Learned From Activity Based Costing in the U.S. Automobile Industry

IMPLEMENTING MANAGEMENT INNOVATIONS
Lessons Learned From Activity Based Costing in the U.S. Automobile Industry

by

Shannon W. Anderson
Rice University
Jessie Jones School of Management

S. Mark Young
University of Southern California
Leventhal School of Accounting, Marshall School of Business

KLUWER ACADEMIC PUBLISHERS
Boston / Dordrecht / London

Distributors for North, Central and South America:
Kluwer Academic Publishers
101 Philip Drive
Assinippi Park
Norwell, Massachusetts 02061 USA
Telephone (781) 871-6600
Fax (781) 681-9045
E-Mail < kluwer@wkap.com >

Distributors for all other countries:
Kluwer Academic Publishers Group
Distribution Centre
Post Office Box 322
3300 AH Dordrecht, THE NETHERLANDS
Telephone 31 78 6392 392
Fax 31 78 6546 474
E-Mail < services@wkap.nl >

 Electronic Services < http://www.wkap.nl >

Library of Congress Cataloging-in-Publication Data

Anderson, Shannon W.
  Implementing management innovations : lessons learned from
activity based costing in the U.S. automobile industry / by
Shannon W. Anderson, S. Mark Young.
        p. cm.
Includes bibliographical references and index.
  ISBN 0-7923-7437-1 (alk. paper)
  1. Activity-based costing--United States. 2. Managerial
accounting--United States. 3. Automobile industry and
trade--United States--Accounting. I. Young, S. Mark. II. Title.
  HF5686.C8 A6847 2001
  629.2'068'1--dc21

2001038128

Printed on acid-free paper.
Printed in the United States of America

*The publisher offers discounts on this book for course use and bulk purchases.
For further information, send email to <david.cella@wkap.com>.*

to our families

Contents

ix

List of Figures

List of Tables

About the Authors

Shannon W. Anderson

Shannon W. Anderson is an Associate Professor of Accounting at the Jesse H. Jones Graduate School of Management, Rice University. She earned a doctorate in Business Economics from Harvard University and a B.S.E. in Operations Research from Princeton University. Her doctoral research received the Institute of Management Accountants' Dissertation Award.

Dr. Anderson's research focuses on designing performance measurement and cost control systems to support management decision-making. Her research has been published in the *Accounting Review, Accounting Organizations and Society, Accounting Horizons, Production and Operations Management* and the *Journal of Management Accounting Research*. Dr. Anderson's research has been supported by grants from the National Science Foundation, The William Davidson Institute, the Institute of Management Accountants, and the International Motor Vehicle Program at M.I.T. She also received an Arthur Andersen Fellowship while at the University of Michigan.

Professor Anderson currently serves on the editorial boards of *Accounting Organizations and Society, The Accounting Review,* the *Journal of Management Accounting Research* and *Management Accounting Research.*

S. Mark Young

S. Mark Young is the KPMG Foundation Professor of Accounting and Professor of Management and Organization at the Marshall School of Business, University of Southern California. Professor Young received an A.B. from Oberlin College and a Ph.D. from the University of Pittsburgh. His articles appear in *The Accounting Review, Accounting, Organizations and Society,* the *Journal of Management Accounting Research,* the *Journal of Accounting Research,* the *Academy of Management Review,* and the *Journal of Marketing Research.* Currently, he serves on the editorial boards of *Accounting, Organizations and Society, and Management Accounting Research,* and is past Associate Editor of *The Accounting Review* and the *Journal of Management Accounting Research.*

Professor Young has received research grants from the National Science Foundation and the Institute of Management Accountants. He has also won four teaching awards. In 1994, Professor Young's coauthored article won the *Notable Contributions to the Management Accounting Literature Award.* In 2001, the third edition of his coauthored textbook, *Management Accounting* and *Readings in Management Accounting* were published by Prentice Hall.

Preface

This book is the result of an in depth study of the implementation of activity based costing (ABC) inside two of America's largest automobile companies. The book extends previous research on ABC implementation by documenting the genesis of ABC at both firms' corporate levels and determining how ABC was rolled out into their plants. One of the distinguishing features of the study is the development of models at both the individual and team levels designed to test specific hypotheses related to implementation success. Information for the study was gathered using a variety of research methods including interviews, surveys and intra-company memos and data.

We are grateful to the Foundation for Applied Research (*FAR*) of the Institute of Management Accountants (*IMA*), the International Motor Vehicle Program (*IMVP*) at the Massachusetts Institute of Technology, Arthur Andersen Company, the University of Michigan Business School, and the Leventhal School of Accounting, Marshall School of Business at the University of Southern California for their financial support.

A number of individuals were instrumental in the access and cooperation that we enjoyed at the research sites: Ken Geddes, Charles McGill, David Galley and Jayne Sheffield at General Motors; and, Ricardo Hernandez, David Mike Novak, David Meador, Mark Newton and Julie Matuszewski at Chrysler. Hundreds of employees at both GM and Chrysler gave graciously of their time to help us understand the local implementation of activity based costing. Julian Freedman, former Research Director of *Foundation of Applied Research* at the *IMA*, was a friend and a source of encouragement throughout the project, and Nick Dousmanis, Terri Funk, John Barry, James Horsch and Robert C. Miller of the IMA have carried on Julian's support. In addition, we thank our colleagues Stan Abraham, Dan Daly and Sandy Rice for helping us gather data at the plants and Teresa Colony who served as our project coordinator. In particular we thank Jim Hesford who assisted us in data collection and analysis and also coauthored Chapter 5.

Portions of this monograph were presented at research workshops at Boston College, Harvard Business School, Michigan State University, Northwestern University, the Stanford Summer Camp, University of Iowa, Memphis State University, the University of Rochester, University of Southern California, University of Washington, and Washington University. We are grateful to all of our colleagues, especially Bob Kaplan, for their comments on our work.

We also thank Anthony Hopwood and Anthony Atkinson for allowing us to use material previously published in *Accounting, Organizations and Society* and the *Journal of Management Accounting Research*. Thanks are also due to David Cella, our editor for his encouragement on the project and Denise Gibson and Judith Pforr for their very able technical assistance. Finally, we thank our families for their constant encouragement and support as we conducted this study.

Chapter 1

INTRODUCTION

1. OVERVIEW

Managers have always experimented with ways to increase employee motivation and organizational performance, however, judging from the popular business press, it appears that management innovation has accelerated dramatically over the past 20 years. By "management innovation" we refer to changes to work practices (as opposed to work outputs) designed to increase organizational performance, defined broadly to include productivity, profitability, product quality and customer satisfaction. Examples include total quality management (TQM), benchmarking best business practices and reengineering existing processes to reflect best practice and supplier management.

Recently, the focus of innovation has shifted from the factory floor to "back office" administrative functions. Often these administrative process innovations are enabled by information technology. For example, enterprise resource planning (ERP) systems replace dispersed, disconnected databases with a common database to form a central nervous system for the firm; similarly, electronic data interchange (EDI) systems create common information protocols between firms and their suppliers or customers and have been associated with reductions in inventory and delivery errors.

In our study of management innovation we have come to believe that the only source of sustainable competitive advantage is the management of knowledge creation -- the "organizational software" of a firm. Firms with innovative management practices are often willing to open their doors to visitors because their organizational software, the real source of their competitive advantage, cannot be easily grasped or imitated. Organizations manage the creation and use of knowledge by developing and retaining highly skilled employees and by providing these employees with appropriate tools that stimulate new insights about routine practices. Management innovations that have emerged in the last two decades truly reflect the emergence of the "knowledge worker" and the information economy -- in which workers are now armed with new information and tools for stimulating new inquiry. Thus, "management" is the task of managing people and their acquisition of knowledge rather than digesting data and issuing marching orders.

Although these trends are encouraging and have been touted as one explanation of contemporaneous growth in the U.S. economy, recent reports by consulting firms, researchers, and the business press, find very mixed results concerning the success of these management innovations. By some accounts, one-third or fewer of these innovations continue after a year.[1] In contrast to positive returns to investments in factory technology, studies of returns to investments in information technology frequently find *negative* returns to management information systems.[2] These reports are particularly troublesome when one considers the millions of dollars invested in implementing these programs as well as the negative impact of fad programs on employee productivity and morale. This sentiment is evident in Thurow's (1987) remark, "The American factory works. The American office doesn't."

There is a great deal of speculation about the causes of innovation success and failure, but few systematic attempts have been made to understand how management innovations aimed at improving knowledge creation and management are adopted and implemented by organizations. In this book we analyze adoption and implementation of a major management innovation of the 1980s and 1990s, activity based costing and activity-based management (ABC/M), by two large firms in the U.S. automobile industry, General Motors and Daimler/Chrysler Corporation. ABC/M is an approach to assigning the costs of firm input resources to firm outputs in a manner that better approximates the causal link between resource provision and resource consumption. It is intended to provide more accurate assessments of the cost of business processes and products; however, perhaps more importantly, it is intended to stimulate insights into costs that generate improvement activities.

This case study of ABC/M implementation provides relevant insights for the broad class of managerial innovations that employ information technology to improve business performance through process improvement. The activity analysis underlying ABC/M can change the way that organizations view their operations and how they measure themselves. Generating ABC data and using the data to create new knowledge about processes is often accompanied by a host of behavioral reactions by the individuals and groups that perform the processes. ABC is more than an isolated modification to an accounting system; it cuts across the organization, determining the estimated cost of every business operation -- both in the factory and in the office. Many popular managerial innovations have attempted to mobilize managers and workers across functional boundaries in the face of natural human resistance to change. Our case study speaks to the unique challenges therein. In sum, understanding ABC implementation may provide a road map not only for companies interested in adopting ABC but also for those who are interested in adopting other management innovations.

2. BACKGROUND FOR THE STUDY

Over fifteen years ago, ABC systems were identified in innovative firms and received widespread coverage in the business literature. With the emergence of lean manufacturing methods and the rapid growth of service operations, activity based costs were viewed as a means of making outdated cost accounting data more relevant for decisions that confronted modern managers. Specifically, activity based costing systems provided cost information that more closely traced resource costs to the business processes (or activities) and products that consumed resources. The focus on costs of business processes caused activity based costing to fit well with another popular innovation of the period, "business process re-engineering."

In the early 1990's, as researchers were codifying a conceptual framework for ABC and many firms were experimenting with ABC systems, the *Institute of Management Accountants (IMA)* sponsored an innovative research program that brought together practitioners and leading academics to study the ABC adoption process. The program, which examined case studies of eight early adopters of ABC, culminated in the award-winning monograph, *Implementing Activity-based Cost Management: Moving from Analysis to Action* (Cooper et al. 1992). The monograph examined circumstances that make ABC attractive to firms, documented the structure of ABC models, and developed recommendations for implementing ABC to achieve maximum benefits from the resulting system. A conclusion of the study was that the adoption of activity based cost management differs from many accounting system changes, in that it makes possible new ways of managing the business. However, the existence of an ABC system is a necessary but not a sufficient condition for these new management methods to arise. Managers must recognize the latent possibilities and be determined to use the information in different ways for activity based management to arise out of activity based costing data.

Cooper et al. focused on the firm's ABC adoption decision and most of the cases focused on the process by which the firms developed their first ABC model. Consistent with the wisdom of the time, most firms that were experimenting with ABC were doing so in a small, somewhat contained part of the organization, using stand-alone personal computers and accepting as inputs data from existing information systems. While these approaches are ideal for testing the viability and usefulness of the ABC concept and for informing the ABC adoption decision, they present problems when the firm contemplates firm-wide "rollout" of ABC. Issues that arise with the management of a firm-wide rollout of ABC include:

- How is the rollout process managed across multiple locations?
- What is the level of involvement needed by employees at plants?
- How are ABC project teams selected and organized?
- How should the ABC system relate to existing information systems (including the traditional cost accounting systems)?
- How do organizational, individual and interpersonal factors associated with the ABC project team influence project outcomes such as model accuracy?
- What kinds of success measures can one use to judge ABC implementation?
- What defines effectiveness, or "success" of an ABC implementation project and how does the answer to the preceding question change with different measures of success?

In an effort to document how firms are answering these questions, in 1992 we set out to conduct a two-phase study of the process of implementing ABC in large organizations. Senior managers of the Big Three were contacted to participate in the first phase of this study. The objectives of the first phase of the research were to understand the emergence of corporate intent to adopt activity based costing. General Motors and Chrysler (now Daimler Chrysler) agreed to be part of the study. Ford declined saying that although ABC was under consideration, there was no immediate plan to adopt it. The goal of the first phase of research was to construct a narrative history of the ABC implementation decision at both firms. This phase relied primarily on interviews and archival records.

General Motors began investigating ABC in 1986 and adopted ABC as a corporate initiative in 1989. Chrysler began investigating ABC in 1989 and developed a plan for corporate-wide implementation in 1992. Both GM and Chrysler were rolling out ABC but were taking somewhat different paths to firm-wide implementation. However, lest this be construed as an inquiry into "the one right way" to implement ABC, both firms experienced what they described as implementation successes and failures. Thus, we knew from the outset that we must go beyond the firm's ABC implementation program and study local ABC implementation projects.

In Phase 2 we collected data from 21 ABC implementation sites. Following the conclusions of Cooper et al., we hypothesized that the academic literatures on organizational change, project management and the implementation of information technology would prove fruitful in framing our inquiry. Consistent with the propositions advanced by Cooper et al., we found that ABC implementation demands significant organizational change. The influential factors in effecting the organizational change associated with ABC implementation are similar to those that have been widely documented in hundreds of studies of other organizational changes. In sum, the bad news is that implementing activity based cost management in a large organization is a daunting task of enacting organizational change at all levels of the firm. The good news is that we have a roadmap of what awaits the firm that attempts to surmount the obstacles and as a result can develop tactical plans for a firm-wide rollout of ABC that anticipates these pitfalls. More generally, in that ABC implementation is one example of a managerial innovation that demands organizational change, this book provides a window on issues surrounding organizational change that applies to many managerial innovations, particularly the broad class of innovations that involve information technology.

We found that the nature and the intensity of the demands that implementation places on the local site are highly dependent on local managers' expectations for the ABC system. Those who would simply obtain more accurate product costs can do so relatively quickly, with little disruption to normal operations, using a project team with good technical knowledge of the organization and strong accounting skills. Those who wish to effect more fundamental change in the management process, for example reorienting decisions around business processes, must employ a multi-disciplinary team of committed change agents with technical knowledge of the organization, superb communications skills and strong support from the full management team. We found considerable disagreement within specific ABC implementation sites as to which objective was desired; this lack of consensus about project goals destined the resulting ABC system to failure in the minds of some managers. The managerial implication is that a major role for any corporate group that supports ABC implementations in disparate corners of the firm is to establish and communicate the firm's strategic objective for the system. The challenge is that this objective is likely to change as the firm gains expertise with and discovers new uses for ABC data; and a change in the firm's strategic objectives for ABC necessitates a review of the implementation and system maintenance strategy.

This book is organized as follows. In Appendix 1 we discuss the details of our research program including how we selected sites and critical informants. We also outline specific field research methods including our interview and survey, and data analysis methods. In Chapter 2 we summarize the literature on ABC implementation, identifying contributions of other studies and highlighting gaps in our knowledge that we strive to address with this research. In Chapter 3 we present a brief narrative history of both firms' decision to adopt ABC. We then describe the strategy that each firm adopted to deploy ABC across hundreds of geographically dispersed, substantively different business operations. Finally, we present the framework originally developed in Anderson (1995) as one way of thinking about the process of ABC implementation and the challenges associated with each stage of deployment.[3] A major component of both firms' rollout plans was the use of an ABC design team to develop and install ABC at each remote site. In Chapter 4 we discuss how ABC team members were chosen, the composition of the teams and implications for management innovation team design. Chapter 5 takes us inside the multi-disciplinary ABC design team and examines how the workings of the team influence outcomes of the ABC implementation project. In Chapter 6 we expand our inquiry to include the perspectives of all of the functional managers at the local site. The focus of this chapter is examining whether existing models of the determinants of effective organizational change fit the experiences of our 21 ABC implementation sites. In Chapter 7 we deconstruct this question by asking what "effective" organizational change means, from the perspective of the managers and ABC team members who participated in our study. Upon discovering widely differing viewpoints on this issue, we revisit our model of effective organizational change to ask whether different factors are implicated in different concepts of effective ABC implementation. We summarize our findings in Chapter 8 and in Chapter 9 discuss the current state of ABC systems in both firms.

3. KEY FINDINGS

3.1 Multi-generation ABC Systems

Implementation of activity based cost management in large firms is associated with significant organizational change. By nature, the development of an ABC model requires the marriage of detailed organization-specific knowledge and knowledge of the theoretical and conceptual model of activity based costing. As a result, large companies typically adopt a sequential strategy of implementing ABC at disparate sites using a team of local experts who have access to (and may be joined by) ABC specialists. A sequential, and in some cases multi-generational (depending on the lags between early and late ABC adopters), strategy is often dictated by scarcity and costs of ABC specialists and by limited capacity of the firm to support parallel projects. One challenge of managing the sequential rollout of ABC is that at any given point, different sites have different levels of experience with and expertise in using ABC data and as a result place different demands for support on the central administration. One firm in our study eventually separated implementation support from maintenance support in recognition of these differences.

Another challenge is that the objectives for ABC may shift in the course of the rollout as the firm gains expertise with ABC and discovers new applications for the data. We find that determinants of "successful" implementation of ABC depend critically on the objectives of the project. Thus, to the extent that firm objectives for ABC change over time, the implementation process must be continually evaluated to insure the alignment of project resources with organizational objectives for each generation of new implementation projects.

3.2 The Work Of The ABC Design Team

ABC training for team members strongly influences the perceived significance of the ABC model development task as does the level of competition each plant faces. As these perceptions of task significance and the ability to resolve group conflicts increase so does the level of ABC team cohesion. Three factors affect the complexity of the ABC model developed -- the presence of an external ABC consultant, the level of outside competition and the ability to resolve group conflicts. While the degree of model complexity does not significantly affect the time to complete the model, a higher level of team cohesion leads to greater speed in developing the first ABC model. A key lesson from our study of ABC teams is that management should not only carefully train employees in why ABC (or any management innovation) is important to them and their organization, but must also develop a work environment by which team cohesion can flourish.

3.3 The Staffing Of The ABC Design Team

On average, it took the sites in our study 7 months to develop an initial ABC model; however this average conceals differences in staffing and model complexity (e.g., the number of business processes and products at the site) that influenced project completion. Left to staff an ABC project with local resources in a climate of constrained headcount, local managers typically did not comply with the recommendation to use a dedicated, multi-disciplinary team. This might cause some to argue that we have not studied "best practice" in ABC implementation. Nevertheless, we believe that our sites are representative of situations that arise when the benefits of ABC implementation accrue primarily to the firm while the costs of ABC implementation reside primarily at local sites. The managerial implication of

8

this is that firms need to subsidize initial implementation to achieve the desired results or make a stronger case for the benefits of ABC data for local managers.

NOTES

[1] Reports vary across innovations, with consultants saying that only 1/3 of TQM initiatives continue after two years. Some ABC consultants estimate that only 10% of ABC programs last.

[2] Brynjolfsson and Yang (1996); Brynjolfsson (1993); and Bakos and Kemerer (1992) provide comprehensive reviews of the literature on returns to IT investment.

[3] Anderson (1995) presents detailed evidence that this model is a reasonable representation of the adoption and implementation process. Krumweide (1998) provides statistical evidence that supports Anderson's hypothesis, that different factors are associated with the successful navigation of each stage of ABC implementation.

Appendix I

THE DESIGN OF THE RESEARCH PROGRAM

1. OVERVIEW

Our program of research has three distinctive characteristics compared to previous research. We believed that using a more intensive, multi-site field research method (as opposed to a mail survey of many firms) would more effectively advance our knowledge of ABC implementation (see Young, 1999 for more discussion). The costs of field research and the time to develop relationships with corporate partners limited our investigation to a small number of firms. Second, we interview and survey multiple users of ABC systems in the same organizations with the goal of understanding the process of ABC model development. Third, over several years, we were able to trace ABC development at both the corporate and plant levels. Extensive interviews were conducted with senior management in both companies and archival information such as internal company memos, etc. We also provide an analysis of plant-level ABC teams, and the factors that lead them to perform the task of developing ABC models. Apart from the advantage of being able to spend a great deal of time inside both companies, we were also able to incorporate archival information into our discussion and analyses and employ many state-of-the-art tools of academic research to conduct our study.

1.1 The Deployment of ABC to Local Sites

A paradox that emerged in Anderson's (1995) research on the emergence of corporate ABC initiatives was that in spite of the importance of successful plant-level prototypes to the firm's decision to adopt ABC, continued corporate support of the ABC initiative did not depend upon 'success' of subsequent ABC projects. Rather, following a period of controlled experimentation when project success was critical, the corporate initiative acquired a life of its own. This observation is consistent with research on innovation adoption and illustrates a critical distinction between individual and organizational adoption of innovations. Specifically, it is not uncommon for one part of an organization, which originates an innovation, to embrace it, while another part of the organization, for which the innovation is a mandate, rejects it (Van de Ven, 1993).

This finding in the early research motivated the second phase of research, aimed at understanding how the deployment of ABC was proceeding in the local ABC implementation sites against the backdrop of a maturing and changing corporate ABC initiative. In light of our concerns about different factions supporting or opposing ABC, we were particularly interested in selecting a broad range of sites, but not so broad a range that we would be unable to plumb the depths of each site. Previous studies of ABC implementation typically rely on one person's evaluation of an entire firm's ABC system. Our concern is that these evaluations reflect an "average" assessment of potentially widely differing project outcomes and may be biased by a top management perspective. We broached the idea of a site-level study of ABC implementation with the companies in 1994 and upon gaining their support, we collected data from 21 ABC implementation sites (10 at one firm and 11 at the other) during 1995. Chapters 5 through 8 present research results from the study of 21 local ABC implementation projects in General Motors and Chrysler. In the sections that follow we describe the selection of research sites and of critical informants. We also provide information about the methods used to collect data in the form of interviews, surveys and archival records from each site.

1.2 Site Selection

Three criteria were used in selecting ABC projects for study. First, we selected plants that initiated ABC system design after the corporate decision to implement ABC was issued but during different periods of each firm's ABC implementation history. We exclude experimental or prototype projects to avoid confounding routine implementations with those that were linked to the organizational decision to adopt ABC. These prototype implementations were discussed in the first phase of the research. Inclusion of projects from different time periods permitted investigation of temporal aspects of adoption and diffusion in later studies.

A second factor in ABC project selection was an attempt to include sites from all production processes used in automobile manufacturing. Approximately half of the sites selected from each firm produce components that are unlikely to be outsourced (what we term 'core' components), including: major metal stampings, foundry castings, engines, and transmissions. The remaining sites face external competition and produce parts that could be outsourced. Selecting a balance of 'core' and peripheral components sites maximizes variation in external economic circumstances (subject to the limitation that the study occurs within a single industry), and allows us to examine the relation between these contextual factors and evaluations of the ABC system. Recall that our sample of plants consisted of *Core* plants -- those in which the corporation has invested heavily in capital equipment. These plants included major metal stamping, engine and transmission assembly, and foundry castings. The core manufacturing process provides the manufacturing identity of the firm. Core plants are captive to their respective corporations, face little outside competition, and historically have been able to sell almost all products they could produce to the corporation. The relative level of competition that Core plants face is low. The second type of plants are *Non Core* plants are those that produce automobile components. These plants are much more peripheral to the firm, and indeed, some have since been "spun off" as new companies. Both firms in our study have been criticized for excessive vertical integration, and most recently, *Non Core* plants at these firms have faced a great deal of competitive pressure that has resulted in outsourcing and plant closings. Compared to *Core* plants, the relative level of competition at *Non Core* plants is high. The sites were selected to represent as nearly as possible, 'matched pairs' across the firms. Factors considered in matching sites include: process technology; product mix complexity; and, plant and equipment age. In addition to traditional manufacturing sites, the service parts distribution groups of both firms are included. We were unable to obtain a match in one firm for a contiguous stamping and assembly plant that was included for the second firm. Thus the final sample includes eleven sites from one firm and ten sites from the other firm.

A final factor in selecting sites is the perceived success of the ABC project. We require sites that represent the full range of ABC system outcomes from each firm's population of ABC sites. One firm adopted ABC in 1991 and consequently had fewer ABC projects from which to choose. Although we met the first two criteria for plant selection, doing so virtually exhausted the population of ABC implementations. Thus it is unlikely that we were directed toward exceptionally good projects. The second firm adopted ABC in 1989 and had over 150 ABC models at the inception of our study. We were concerned that the above criteria would allow over-sampling of relatively successful ABC projects. To ensure that the firms did not limit the population in this manner, we required an independent assessment of 'success'. As part of the firm-level study, eight division-level ABC managers completed a survey covering 50 ABC plant implementations with which they were familiar. Seven of the ten proposed research sites were among the sites covered by the survey. One question dealt with ABC system success and another dealt with ABC system use by local managers. Responses related to the seven research sites indicated that the sites we were offered represent the full range of success and management use of the ABC system.

As a result, ten corporate and division-level employees were interviewed to document the development of the ABC initiative. Hundreds of pages of internal memos and training materials were reviewed to corroborate and extend the interview data.

1.3 Critical Informants

We gathered data from individuals who were directly involved in the designing the ABC model, as well as from the full management team at the location. The literature on organizational change is clear on two matters. First, organizational change is a process of changing the beliefs and behaviors of individuals. Although key individuals may play a disproportionate role in convincing others to adopt an innovation, it is rare that a single individual can unilaterally adopt innovations on behalf of an organization. Second, the beliefs and behaviors of individuals toward a particular innovation are shaped by their unique, individual circumstances within the organization.[1] Together these observations suggest that variation in the evaluation of ABC systems between different managers from a single plant may be quite large, and that consideration of the opinions of all influential parties is necessary when evaluating the ABC system. It also highlights a potential limitation of previous research that is based on surveys completed by accounting professionals. We use two populations of critical informants: ABC system developers and the site's management team (e.g., the plant manager and functional managers who report to the plant manager).[2]

2. FIELD RESEARCH PROCEDURES

Anyone planning to conduct a field study of this kind has to be aware of the enormous time commitment involved. In total we were involved for three years with our host firms. Three important preliminary events occurred before the study began. First, and perhaps most importantly, we were fortunate to gain entree to the research sites and commitment on the part of the firms to the study. The companies allowed us to conduct the study as they wanted an objective study of ABC implementation.[3] Both companies were very generous with their time and facilitated the study. Second, we spent a total of 18 months planning the study. Planning included several logistical elements: determining who to interview at the corporate and plant levels, deciding which plants to visit and the procedures that we would follow when were inside the plants. Third, we needed to develop survey instruments and an interview procedures that would capture how ABC was perceived by employees. Since no existing instruments were available we had to develop our own. The logistical issues and instruments are described below in more detail.

At the plant level, we employed a project administrator as well as several research assistants. For each plant visit, we followed a standardized procedure. Once a plant site had approved our entry, the project administrator set up our visits. The administrator requested interviews from a list of job titles and sent out a two-day research schedule (See Figure A.1).

Figure A.1: Suggested Plant Schedule

DAY 1: Principal Researchers S. Anderson and S. M. Young

30 min.	1.	Introductory Meeting with Plant Manager and Plant Controller:

Objective: Describe the purpose of our study, answer questions, ask for their ABC-related questions, explain confidentiality policy, and seek general project buy-in. Insure that survey distribution has occurred.

1 hour	2.	Overview Plant Tour: led by an experienced engineer or first line supervisor. Preferably *not* an ABC team member

4 hours	3.	Interview ABC team members: original and maintenance teams Lunch with ABC team members at a natural break in interviews Collect self-administered surveys

1 hour	4.	Interview Plant Controller

Research Assistant:

	1.	Sets up area for survey collection and ABC archival records (needs frequent access to copy machine)
	2.	Catalogue self-administered surveys
	3.	Collect and catalogue archival data from ABC system and implementation process

DAY 2: Principal Researchers: S. W. Anderson and S. M. Young

3.5 hours	1.	Interview Managers of Major Functional areas:

    a.   Industrial Engineering., Manufacturing Engineering., Management Information Systems, Material Management, Production Operations. (30 minutes each)

    b.   Collect Surveys and answer any questions concerning survey

    c.   Interview with Manager of Production Operations should be scheduled as early as possible to allow student time to catalogue larger number of surveys collected in this interview.

1 hour	2.	Researchers lunch with research assistant to assess progress and revise strategy for completing plant data collection if necessary

1 hour	3.	Interview with plant cost accountants individually (20-30 minutes each)

1 hour	4.	Interview plant manager and controller

	5.	Review archival data collected by student and assess survey yield

About a week prior to our visit, the administrator sent a packet of information to the plant including two types of surveys and a plant statistics questionnaire (details of all instruments are discussed below). One survey was designed for ABC team members and the other for functional managers. Since a large part of our research design focused on perceptual differences in ABC implementation there were a number of overlapping questions posed to functional members and ABC team members. In addition, we included questions tailored to each group. We asked that respondents fill out the surveys prior to our arrival. Surveys were collected from respondents before each was interviewed. In some cases surveys were sent back to us if they had not been completed.

For each plant at least one of the principal researchers and one research assistant conducted the study. In many cases the principal researchers visited each plant. At the beginning of each plant visit, the principal researchers and the research assistant would meet with the plant manager and plant controller to outline our plans for the visit and to address any questions. Next, the research team would go on a plant tour that was usually conducted by an industrial engineer. Each tour lasted about an hour depending on the size of the plant. The plant tours were designed to familiarize us with products produced, the processes employed and their sequence, and the organizational setting.

Once the plant tour ended we began our interview schedule. Interviews followed a standard format and we designed questions for the various types of individuals that we interviewed. For example, we used a series of questions for functional managers, the plant controller, the plant manager and for ABC team members. While we were conducting interviews, the research assistant began to gather archival information and to go over the plant statistics questionnaire with the ABC team leader who was charged with filling it out. At the end of each plant visit, we met again with the plant manager and controller to discuss any lingering questions. We did not discuss any specifics of what we had observed at each plant given the confidentiality agreements that we specified with each organizational participant.

2.1 Data Collection Instruments

The data collection effort for this project was extensive. Multiple research methods including archival information, interview data, survey data and direct observation were used to collect a wide variety of data.

2.1.1 The Survey Instruments

Two comprehensive surveys were developed, one for ABC team members (*Survey of Activity Based Costing Implementation* - hereafter, *ABC Team Survey*) ABC and the other for managers (*Management Survey of Activity Based Costing Implementation* - hereafter, *Manager Survey*). These surveys are reprinted in Appendices 2 and 3. Items for the surveys were taken developed in two ways. First, given the model of implementation that we developed, we used scales or portions of scales that had already been developed in the literature.[4] In some cases wording changes had to be made to be consistent with the organizational context. Second, since many of the constructs that we needed were unique to the study, we had to develop these using information gathered during the pre-study phase. We administered a pre-test of the two surveys to approximately ten corporate and divisional ABC employees (all with prior experience implementing ABC in manufacturing sites) for each company. After administering the surveys, we reviewed item wording with special attention to those developed specifically for this study. The pre-test helped us to identify and correct ambiguous questions.

We also collected other information about the plants such as: 1) plant size, 2) product and process complexity, and 3) environmental turbulence, as well as information about the ABC models developed. As a supplement to both questionnaires the plants were asked to provide a plant layout with geographically distinct activity centers clearly marked.

2.1.2 Archival Data Collection

Archival data collection included: (1) ABC Reports and distribution, (2) existing cost accounting reports & distribution, (3) parameters of ABC model-original and maintenance/revision models, (4) Memos/ meeting minutes issued regarding ABC: from team, plant management, corporate and (5) training seminar schedule and attendance the number of products produced, number of vendors, etc. The ABC Site Coordinator was asked to gather as much information as possible before our visit. Examples of archival records include:

- manuals related to ABC system design or skill training (e.g. activity dictionaries other design templates, software training manuals)
- reports generated from the ABC system and a list of recipients
- memoranda, personal notes, spreadsheets or presentation materials that document the development of the first ABC system and subsequent revisions, the diffusion of ABC concepts, or the use of ABC data.

The research assistant also was responsible for discussing the implementation with the lead ABC developer. This discussion was designed to trigger the lead's memory regarding archival information that may have been played a critical role during the implementation. The research assistant was also given license at each plant to look through the ABC files for other types of information. Searching the archival records varied in difficulty based on the age of the ABC system, the job continuity of ABC implementers and whether implementers had kept a good set of records.

2.1.3 Interview Data

On average we conducted approximately 15 semi-structured interviews per plant each lasting 30 minutes with managers having indirect ABC implementation involvement and ultimate usage responsibility (Industrial Engineering, Manufacturing Engineering, Management Information Systems, Materials Management, Production Operations Superintendent). We concluded each visit with a brief wrap-up session with the plant manager and controller. Although, in keeping with our confidentiality agreements, we did not discuss details of our visit to their plant, we did answer questions regarding the purpose and projected output of our study.

We asked to interview all functional managers who report directly to the plant manager, the plant manager, all people with past or present responsibility for ABC system development or maintenance, and any other people with direct or indirect responsibility for the ABC system or its use. As a result of absenteeism, scheduling conflicts, or job turnover among ABC implementers, we were able to interview 206 of the 265 survey respondents.

Interviews with functional managers, ABC implementers, and other "critical users" of ABC data were intended to supplement survey data and to provide an oral history of the plant's ABC implementation. Interviews began with the collection of the written survey and a brief explanation of the research project. The independence of the researchers and the confidentiality of both the surveys and interviews were discussed and permission was sought to tape the interview. In only two cases of 206 interviews was permission to tape the interview denied, with "discomfort with taping" as the reason for denial. In one case the respondent was subsequently found to have little knowledge of the local ABC project. In the second case the respondent was a member of the original ABC implementation team and was a critical informant for the site. In both cases the interview proceeded with the researcher taking written notes.

During the first part of the interview, respondents were asked to describe their job responsibilities and their work history. They were then asked to recount the history of the plant's implementation of ABC. We used methods developed by Fisher and Geiselman (1992) on eyewitness testimony to enhance respondent recall of distant events.

3. DATA ANALYSIS

Survey data are analyzed using statistical methods such as: regression analysis, analysis of variance (ANOVA), structural equation modeling, partial least squares (PLS). Where appropriate, interview data are quantified using a content analysis program and analyzed using statistical methods. In other cases, rich descriptions from the interviews are presented directly to the reader to retain the voice of the manager in our research. In balancing statistical analysis with presentations of qualitative interview data we hope to present a rich story of multi-generational deployment of ABC in large organizations that is both convincing and thought provoking. For readability, we limit our discussion of data analysis methods and refer the interested reader to research papers where these details are well documented.

NOTES

[1] See Pedhazur and Schmelkin (1991) for a discussion of respondent effects associated with factors such as age, gender, and educational attainment, as well as a variety of personality traits.

[2] Although some have argued that effective use of ABC requires involvement of employees at the lowest level of the organization, the firms of this study have not disseminated ABC data to this audience. Thus we have no basis for investigating the associations between workers' attitudes and ABC system outcomes and were discouraged from doing so by both firms. Production workers are occasionally included in the survey population as ABC system developers when they served on development teams.

[3] We neither asked for, nor received, compensation for this project from either company to maintain our objectivity. We were fortunate to receive funding for travel and administrative expenses from the sponsors listed in the acknowledgements to this monograph.

[4] See Van de Ven (1980); Seashore et al., (1983); McLennan (1989); Robinson et al. 1991); Davis (1989); Davis, et al. (1989) and Jaworski and Young (1992).

Chapter 2

WHAT WE KNOW (AND DON'T KNOW) ABOUT ABC IMPLEMENTATION

1. THE GENESIS OF ACTIVITY BASED COSTING

In the business literature, emphasis on business activities and processes can be traced to Michael Porter's (1980) "value chain" framework for analyzing sources of firms' competitive advantage. During the same time period, Porter's colleagues at Harvard Business School, Robin Cooper and Robert Kaplan, discovered firms that had modified traditional cost accounting systems to better represent the flow of resources to the products and services that consumed them. Traditional costing systems are typically designed to allocate overhead costs from the general ledger to an entity with reporting responsibility (e.g., profit centers, cost centers, or investment centers) and from that entity to the products or services that it produces. The latter allocation of overhead costs to products is typically accomplished by prorating overhead costs on the basis of direct labor hours, material costs, or another measure of unit variable costs.

The cost systems that Cooper and Kaplan identified bore a strong resemblance to Porter's value chain --- with overhead costs traced from the general ledger to a *business activity*. Business activities often cross boundaries of the reporting and responsibility structure of the organization. Moreover, unlike traditional systems, activity costs were subsequently traced to products or services that place demands on the activity using "cost drivers" to assign costs in proportion to the level of demand for the activity. In documenting these systems, Kaplan and Cooper constructed a theory of resource consumption and suggested an approach, known as *activity based costing* (ABC) for representing resource provision and consumption in cost accounting systems. These representations led to prescriptions for managing the firm's value chain through *activity based management* (ABM).

The earliest activity based costing (ABC) systems were developed to overcome distortions in product costs caused by traditional two-stage costing systems.[1] In traditional cost systems, overhead costs such as indirect labor, utilities, and maintenance supplies are allocated to "burden" centers that typically mirror the reporting and responsibility structure of the organization. Costs from burden centers are allocated to products, typically using a single, unit volume-based, cost driver such as direct labor cost. The key assumption that gives rise to cost distortions is that resources are consumed in direct proportion to the number of units of a product that are produced. For resources such as direct labor, the proportional-use assumption is often appropriate. For almost all support and indirect resources (e.g., production supplies or utilities) the proportional-use assumption leads to inappropriate allocations.

Intuitively, products vary in the activities required to produce them and in the intensity with which they use resources. One product may require a great deal of material handling, several machine setups and hours of machine time while another product uses a small amount of material handling, one setup and half an hour of machine time. Traditional costing systems do not reflect these differences because overhead costs are pooled in a burden center and allocated using a basis that rarely bears any relation to the intensity with which products consume resources in the burden center. Activity based costing mitigates distortions in product costs by assigning costs to activity centers and to products using cost drivers that bear a strong causal relation to resource consumption. Moreover, by organizing costs around business activities rather than the reporting and responsibility structure of the organization, ABC facilitates value chain analysis as well as efforts to re-engineer business processes for efficiency. This strategic use of ABC data, termed activity based management, has revolutionized the field of management accounting, elevating cost analysis from a tactical exercise in management evaluation and control to a key component of strategic planning.

Distorted product costs motivated many firms to redesign their product cost systems. The focus on product costing meant that most early adopters of ABC were manufacturing firms, for whom product costing and inventory valuation were necessary obligations of the accounting system. Cooper and Kaplan used descriptive cases of specific ABC systems to formulate a theoretical framework that reconciles resource provision and consumption and that relates cost accounting systems to critical business processes. In so doing, they demonstrated the relevance of ABC to the larger business enterprise and to a wide array of industry settings, including those of service providers and not-for profit enterprises. Their message was timely; in recent years ABC has emerged in a host of organizations and has been applied to all phases of the production and delivery of products and services.

Today, most managers are aware of activity based costing as a management information tool and many have had direct involvement in the implementation of ABC or have access to ABC data. Technological advances, such as installation of enterprise resource planning systems (ERPs), integration of disparate databases into easily queried "data warehouses," and development of powerful data analysis tools (e.g., data mining software), have facilitated the technical demands that ABC places on organization. However, these advances have generally not dealt with a basic finding of this study --- effective ABC systems are often defined, not by the accuracy of the cost data, but by their ability to answering pressing questions. Technology makes answering questions easier; however, with the exception of chance patterns in data that data mining produces, technology has done very little to insure that managers ask the right questions.

2. WHAT WE KNOW ABOUT ABC IMPLEMENTATION

From the earliest cases describing ABC implementation to more recent descriptions of ABC implementation experience, we have become increasingly aware that developing a cost model that reflects resource consumption is a challenging assignment in socio-technical systems design. One objective of the first IMA monograph was to offer a plan for implementing ABC based on the experiences of eight firms. The resulting plan was overwhelmingly focused on technical steps of model building (e.g., determining the scope of the model, collecting and coding data from a variety of sources, and selecting appropriate cost drivers). Two exceptions, which hinted at the impact of behavioral factors during implementation, were recommendations to use a cross-functional project team and to conduct training at various junctures in the implementation project so that key managers would be equipped to use the ABC data.

Since the IMA monograph was published, there has been increased interest in and acceptance of activity based costing. ABC is a component of most business schools' required curriculum and many schools also offer specialized executive courses for current managers. Most texts in management accounting feature ABC prominently and business conferences on ABC and cost management innovations are common.[2] Large and small consulting firms consider ABC implementation, training and related advisory services as core products. Many of these firms developed specialized computer software to support ABC model development and data analysis. Other software firms that specialize in enterprise resource planning systems, such as SAP® and PeopleSoft®, have developed ABC modules to augment their core financial products.

In spite of what appears to be widespread acceptance of the value of the activity based costing approach, implementation has not been uniformly successful. Although many organizations are satisfied with their ABC systems, others have halted implementation before completion, or abandoned the approach after developing it.[3] In some organizations, cynical observers have reinterpreted the ABC acronym, as "Avoid Being Counted" or "Another Big Cut." These remarks point to the organizational challenges of implementing managerial tools that provide information about the costs of largely unmonitored, administrative work processes. ABC implementation failures in seemingly motivated organizations have spawned articles and books that explore what appear to be the causes of failure and offer advice to those who would avoid similar pitfalls. Titles from the popular press provide vivid indications of the challenges posed by ABC implementation; for example: *Ten Myths About Implementing an Activity-Based Cost System*, and *Activity Based Management: Arthur Andersen's Lessons from the ABM Battlefield.*[4]

2.1 Determinants of Effective ABC Implementation

Researchers have taken a more sober approach to investigating determinants of ABC implementation success, reaching conclusions that are somewhat but not altogether different from those offered in the popular press. In the sections that follow, we discuss two major themes that have emerged from efforts to define critical determinants of effective ABC implementation. The first insight that has emerged in every description of an ABC project is the importance of people to the implementation process. Here we refer to critical roles of those who launch the ABC project, the project team members, and those whose activities are reflected in the ABC model. The second theme, first suggested in the IMA monograph, is the realization that although ABC is a technical information system, it aims to represent and promote change in the social system that is the firm. We cannot evaluate or interpret the success or failure of a particular ABC model strictly by examining the model itself. Stated differently, an ABC model cannot be divorced from the context in which it was created. Following is a more detailed discussion of how these factors influence the outcomes of ABC implementation projects.

2.1.1 The People Guiding the Process

2.1.1.1 Advocacy, Sponsorship and ABC Champions[5]

Like most management innovations, the genesis of most ABC implementations can be traced to an *advocate* or *champion*. Champions emerge from various parts of the organization but most often come from Finance or Manufacturing. Those who provide critical support for the ABC project are known as *sponsors*. Champions are key figures for successful implementation, and a recent survey conducted by Foster and Swenson (1997) found that respondents rated the ABC champion as the individual most responsible for the success of ABC.

The champion's role is to galvanize the organization into action by *gaining the support of senior management*, *securing the necessary organizational resources* through the sponsor and mobilizing and educating the people who will implement and use the system. A survey by Shields (1997) of 143 individuals indicates that gaining top management support for any ABC effort is the most important factor for successful implementation.[6]

Top management support provides the legitimacy and authority needed for many in an organization to take a management innovation seriously.

Organizational support for the champion often depends on his or her political capital, the presence of sponsors, and an ability to convince organizational participants of the value of ABC. Anecdotally, ABC initiatives arising from the Finance organization may be viewed with skepticism by manufacturing personnel. Buying into the initiative may depend on the history of relations between these areas. For instance, ABC is often perceived by manufacturing as a method for analyzing activities with the goal of greater efficiency and lower costs. Since manufacturing knows the most about the production process, they believe that they should have a strong voice in these investigations. While the proportion of champions that come from different functional areas is uncertain, many do come from Finance.[7] Seventy-eight percent (130/166) of the surveys in Foster and Swenson's ABC implementation were completed by individuals from Finance and Accounting. The recommendation in Cooper et al., that the champion should form a multidisciplinary ABC development team that cuts across functional boundaries, seems a prudent approach to address some of these turf battles. Ironically, the attention to cost reduction and efficiency that prompts a firm to implement ABC is often the reason that smaller teams of individuals from finance are charged with implementation. For example, at our research sites, in times of intense cost pressure it was difficult for managers to spare knowledgeable people from manufacturing and other operational areas for administrative initiatives.

2.1.1.2 Multidisciplinary ABC Development Teams

The task of the *multidisciplinary ABC development team* is to develop and implement an ABC model of their facility. At a fundamental level, we know that the team's responsibility includes linking resources to activities and then assigning activity costs to products based on cost drivers. But the successful functioning of the team is often contingent on other factors, such as the political power of the champion, top management support and support for the benefits of ABC. The IMA monograph is the only study we found that discusses characteristics of ABC development teams: for three research sites[8] the process of team member selection and training is described. The subsequent literature has not progressed beyond the stage of recommending that team members be knowledgeable about ABC, comfortable with the technology, and that together, team members represent the full range of critical organizational functions. No study to date has provided a penetrating look at interpersonal and task-related factors that might cause a team to be more or less effective in designing the ABC model. In this book we attempt to shed light on how the workings of the team critically affect project outcomes.

2.2 Resistance to ABC

Understanding and overcoming *resistance* to management innovations such as ABC can be the most challenging aspect of implementation. The overriding reasons for individual resistance to ABC are: inadequate understanding of the theory and benefits of ABC; low tolerance for change; perceived (or real) threats related to job security, compensation, or management control; and beliefs that the ABC model is inaccurate or unable to provide data for particular management issues.

2.2.1 Education: Understanding the Theory and Benefits of ABC

Educating organizational participants about the efficacy and benefits of ABC is a critical part of successful change. Argyris and Kaplan (1994) argue that ABC is similar to other technical theories of action and change such as total quality management (TQM). They discuss necessary steps to help organizational participants overcome resistance to change. The first step is to convince organizational participants that ABC is an internally consistent theory. This means that different managers should be able to apply the theory to a particular problem and obtain similar results. The second step is to illustrate the theory's external validity. Managers should be able to make a decision with ABC information with predictable consequences.

2.2.2 Organizational Tolerance of Change

Over time, organizations develop shared values and behavioral norms. In some cases a "collective mindset" becomes a central part of an organization's culture. One aspect of organizational culture that is particularly relevant for ABC implementers is the degree to which an organization is open to change. Studying an organization's history of management innovations and their subsequent outcomes is one means of detecting whether an organization has a low tolerance for change. Outcomes of historical projects often predict outcomes of future innovation programs because organizational participants rarely understand the cause of the failure, and as a result, often repeat their errors.[9] For example, Young (1997) believe that an important precondition for ABC implementation success is previous experience with other process-oriented improvement programs such as total quality management methods or just-in-time approaches to inventory reduction. When we encounter employees who speak of ABC as the "acronym of the month" it is unlikely that the organization has convinced its employees that any innovation is meaningful or important. This issue echoes Argyris and Kaplan's claims that education about any management innovation is a critical precursor to acceptance of the change.

In some cases, the current *structure of an organization* may also impede implementation success. Using data from a survey of individuals of 162

Canadian strategic business units, Gosselin (1997) provides evidence to resolve a paradoxical issue regarding ABC adoption versus implementation. He finds that organizations that are vertically differentiated (e.g., having a large number of hierarchical levels below the CEO) are more likely *to adopt* ABC. The reason is that ABC is considered an administrative rather than technical innovation and that administrative innovations are more consistently adopted in bureaucratic organizations. However, those organizations that are more *centralized* (decision making is concentrated at one level of an organizational hierarchy and *formalized* (jobs are standardized within an organization) are more likely *to fully implement* ABC. Gosselin argues that this is because these organizations have less flexibility to halt an ABC implementation compared to those that are decentralized and informal.

2.2.3 Perceived Threats to Jobs, Compensation and Control

In some cases, even if managers and employees understand the theory and benefits of ABC and if the organization has historically been open to change, specific managers may engage in what Argyris and Kaplan (1994) call *defensive behavior*. Defense behavior arises when managers feel threatened or embarrassed about the likely outcomes of ABC. Defensive behavior is commonly disguised by plausible objections. Player and Keys (1995) identify 30 objections that managers frequently raise throughout ABC implementation.

As an illustration of a situation in which ABC is likely to induce defensive behavior, consider activities associated with material handling. One of the key benefits of ABC is the ability to determine the relative costs of value-added and non-value-added business processes. For many organizations, material handling is necessitated by production operations that are not adjacent to one another or by remote inventory locations. Although these activities are necessary given the current layout of the facility, they are not value-added processes from the perspective of the final customer. If material handling costs are revealed by the ABC analysis to be significant, the ABC team might recommend redesigning the shop floor layout to reduce the length of material movements. With less time spent on each material handling task, it may be possible to reduce the number of employees dedicated to material handling, to dispose of extra equipment, and to reduce the cost of maintaining equipment. Clearly these cost savings could threaten the employment future of employees associated with material handling. Perhaps less evident but potentially as threatening is the erosion of power that material handling managers might experience if the group that they supervise shrinks.

Cobb et al. (1993) report the case of an organization in the United Kingdom that rejected ABC because preliminary analyses showed that using ABC "increased costs for particular product lines" that were favored by certain powerful managers. This example points to a particularly insidious form of defensive behavior that is likely to arise in large, vertically integrated firms. In these settings it is common for one division to supply inputs to another division and for the division managers to be *compensated* based on both divisional and firm performance. If activity based costing moves costs or "profits" (e.g., as calculated against a market price or an imputed transfer prices) between divisions, there will be winners and losers in the transaction who will naturally defend or oppose ABC depending the side of the equation on which they find themselves. Thus, ABC has implications for the design of management compensation and control systems that must be addressed before implementation begins, lest implementation be doomed by conflicting incentives.

2.2.4 Technical Problems with ABC Models

A final set of reasons that managers oppose the implementation of ABC are beliefs that the ABC model does not accurately represent the economics of the organization, is cumbersome to use, or does not provide timely data. ABC models are considered overly complex, not complex enough or are based on the "wrong" activities or cost drivers. Certainly many recent technological advances aimed at integrating information systems and making data access more transparent and intuitive to users will ameliorate these very real problems, However, Cooper et al. posit that these concerns may also be overcome with *involvement of users* throughout the implementation process. Thus, technical and behavioral and organizational problems are often intertwined and cannot be easily separated.

3. WHAT WE DON'T KNOW ABOUT ABC IMPLEMENTATION

Necessarily, early research on ABC implementation was conducted in a case study setting. Researchers focused on innovative firms and used these cases to articulate a conceptual framework of resource consumption in the firm. As ABC entered the mainstream it became possible to move out of the case study setting to investigate widespread phenomena associated with the use of ABC employing data collection methods such as mail surveys and telephone surveys. This progression from case studies aimed at theory development to large sample studies aimed at theory testing is common in academia. However, we believe that the transition from case studies of ABC adoption to large sample surveys of mature ABC implementations was premature. Specifically, we believe that a failure to understand the *maturation process* limits our ability to interpret the large sample results and has artificially created the illusion that we know how to implement activity based costing in large complex organizations. General questions such as "How should a firm-wide rollout of ABC be managed?" and "What are the people issues involved with ABC implementation?" stated in Chapter 1 are extremely difficult to answer without getting directly involved with local ABC projects.

In moving prematurely from case studies of initial ABC models to surveys of large organizations with mature ABC systems, we have failed to address questions that arise when ABC expands from a prototype or "special study" to a management system that is part of the larger organizational bureaucracy. Our purpose in conducting this study is to return to the field to understand how firms are answering these questions and to test the validity of existing models of organizational change and project management for describing the phenomena of mixed success in ABC implementation that so many firms have reported.

NOTES

[1] R. S. Kaplan and R. Cooper's *Cost and Effect* (Harvard Business School Press, 1998) and A. Atkinson et al.'s text, *Management Accounting, 3rd Edition* (Prentice Hall, 2001) provide comprehensive coverage of ABC.

[2] Business conferences include CAM-I, CostCon, CMC2000 and others, which bring leading practitioners together.

[3] See Player and Keys (1995) for examples of success and failure.

[4] See Turney (1992) and Player and Keys (1995).

[5] See Shields and Young (1989) and Argyris and Kaplan (1994) for further discussion.

[6] See Shields and Young (1989); Argyris and Kaplan (1994); Shields (1997); Foster and Swenson (1997) and McGowan and Klammer (1997).

[7] Accounting falls under the Finance umbrella in many organizations.

[8] The sites were Advanced Micro Devices, Monarch Mirror Door Company and Kraft USA.

[9] See Young (1997).

Chapter 3

THE EMERGENCE OF COPORATE ABC INITIATIVES: TOWARDS A MODEL OF ABC IMPLEMENTATION

1. OVERVIEW

This chapter provides a narrative history of the emergence of ABC as a corporate initiative in the firms in our study. A major theme that runs through both accounts is the bureaucratic processes associated with bringing ABC to corporate consciousness and evaluating its potential as a corporate initiative. We use the term "bureaucratic" not in a pejorative sense, but to highlight a major difference between implementing ABC in a small versus a large firm. In a small firm a single ABC model can include all costs and the "pilot" study is the forerunner of the completed model. In a large firm hundreds of ABC models are needed to capture all of the business activities and costs of the firm, and any pilot study of necessity provides only a glimpse of the likely future challenges, costs and benefits of deploying ABC to the full organization. We use our observations at General Motors and Chrysler, as well as literature on the implementation of information technology and cost management change to develop a model of ABC implementation.

The story of General Motors' adoption of ABC is one of a pioneer carefully navigating unknown waters. The story is remarkable primarily because of the degree to which individuals promoted something that they believed would improve cost management practices in an organization that is not known for rewarding risk-taking. The story of Chrysler's adoption begins as one of a prudent follower taking every opportunity to learn from those who went before it and seeking out experienced guides (including General Motors) for the journey. However, before long Chrysler realized that it knew as much about ABC as its advisors and consultants. More importantly, the firm had a clearer understanding about how the ABC initiative needed to mature and become integrated with other information systems than did consultants who were accustomed to selling ABC services in isolation. As a result, early in the deployment process Chrysler took the lead and relegated consultants to being a means to augment the skilled labor force and overcome the initial startup problems of ABC implementation.

Although these stories are intriguing in themselves, it is not our aim to simply add more anecdotes to the ABC literature. Historical data on the emergence of ABC at General Motors was used in Anderson (1995) to propose a theory of the process of ABC implementation. We do not repeat the details of the analysis here, but close with the framework from that study. The key insights from the framework are:

- that the implementation process passes through several stages of development;
- that successful navigation of each stage depends on a combination of technical and social factors; and,
- that the factors that matter differ between stages.

The latter observation, corroborated in a separate study by Krumwiede (1998), is critical because it demands that those responsible for implementing ABC be attentive to the maturation process and responsive to organizational needs at each stage of implementation. In short, it is not enough to launch an ABC implementation project --- it must be shepherded through the rocky passes and ravines associated with system maintenance, adaptation and use.

2. GENERAL MOTORS' ADOPTION OF ABC[1]

During the 1970s, General Motors addressed distortions in product costs caused by allocating manufacturing overhead over a dwindling direct labor base in diverse processing environments by increasing the number of "burden centers" in plants. The Director of Product Cost for North American Operations (NAO) recalled, "we went from one or two burden centers to ... as many as 1200 centers in one production complex." By the 1980s, pressure to outsource component manufacture, coupled with tremendous investments in capital and indirect labor-intensive processes caused managers to question whether this solution led to accurate component costs.

In 1984, a study of costing procedures was launched by the Comptroller's Office. The report recommended augmenting labor-based burden rates with "weights" to reflect process complexity. A member of the study team recalled that what started as a bold initiative to revolutionize product costing ended with a shallow recommendation to adjust the labor-based system. This occurred because the team was overwhelmed by the diversity of costing practices they discovered and the impossible task of developing a universal cost system. There is no evidence that the recommendations were implemented; perhaps because, as one manager described, it was viewed as an incremental solution and it provided no guidance about how the "weights" were to be established.

In the early 1980s investments in transfer presses dramatically reshaped the economic landscape of GM metal stamping facilities.[2] Plants that received these investments were assured a future, but faced substantially different cost structures with high capital costs and increased consumption of indirect support resources. Plants that were not modernized were threatened with closure and faced aggressive outsourcing mandates. The radical shift of fortunes brought about by transfer press technology in conjunction with the acknowledgment by corporate accounting of a "product costing problem" stimulated plant comptrollers to launch experiments in product costing.[3] Although costing experiments emerged in different production facilities, most of the experiments occurred in stamping plants.

In early 1987, five separate, uncoordinated costing experiments were underway; three in metal stamping plants and a fourth originated at GM Research Labs (GMR) but was applied to metal stamping. One stamping plant developed a hybrid system called "factored-piece time" that used direct labor, machine hours and sales dollars to allocate indirect costs to products. A second, modernized plant treated each transfer press as a separate cost center and used machine hours to allocate costs to products. A third plant that had not received transfer presses and was threatened with closure, experimented with an approach called "transactions costing" that was later renamed ABC.[4]

Researchers at GMR were developing an economic model for analyzing transfer press investments when they discovered that the required input data (e.g., machine-level data on setup costs and maintenance) did not exist. The research project was reorganized in 1987, and one task force was charged with assessing sources of cost data and developing better cost information systems. The team formulated a model of a cost matrix with different resource categories as the columns and different operational steps for metal stamping as the rows, a conceptualization that differed from the stamping plants' objective of tracing overhead costs to products. The GMR model was the first recognition of costing "activities" rather than products; and had profound effects later, when ABC was implemented at GM plants that were less concerned about product costs.

Although ABC started as a local initiative, the team was unique among those experimenting with new cost approaches in overtly promoting its activities in the corporation. In early 1987, the plant comptroller (and chief sponsor of the cost system experiment) convened a meeting of all Chevrolet-Pontiac-Canada (CPC, one of four Groups comprising GM NAO at that time) stamping plant comptrollers to share the results of an initial two-product pilot study and to teach them the ABC approach (ABC product costs were not yet available). One team member recalled the strategy of convincing these plants to develop ABC models:

> After the meeting where we introduced the theory to the CPC managers, we sent them periodic progress reports... We even trained one person from [another plant] to develop their pilot ABC model... [the plant

comptroller] told people about our work at every opportunity and a big part of the team leader's job was responding to requests for information.

Two stamping plants were persuaded to try the approach. At the same time, plants from different Groups, including two ACG (Automotive Components Group) plants and an engine plant contacted the team and with their technical support began experimenting with ABC. Moving beyond financial circles, the plant comptroller also publicized ABC in CPC's manufacturing and engineering areas.

As a result of widespread promotion of the ABC experiment, the GMR researchers stumbled across it in mid-1987:

...We'd seen the systems being developed in the other stamping plants. ... they were trying to take the concept of what we now know as ABC and shoehorn it into some sort of adjusted labor hour that reflects differences in parts. So it had a similar philosophy... but it hadn't quite let go of the old idea that everything has to pass through labor hours to be able to allocate dollars to it.

The ABC experiment broke out of the "chart of accounts" framework and was similar to the researchers' cost matrix. Recognizing that the data they sought was not available, and as part of GMR's policy of rotating employees into production jobs to expose them to practical problems, the researchers joined the ABC design team in Fall 1987, to develop an ABC model for the plant's second major production area. This early linkage to a constituency outside of accounting that was knowledgeable about ABC and needed ABC data was to prove invaluable when all of the cost experiments were evaluated at the corporate level.

Nineteen Eighty-Four marked the end of formal Corporate and Group inquiry into new product costing methods; however, Group accounting departments kept close watch over the field experiments. On August 18, 1987 the ABC plant team was invited to present their results to GM's Comptroller and to the CPC Group Director of Finance in a presentation entitled: "CPC Group Transaction Based Costing: An Implementation Proposal."[5] They reviewed the project's objectives--- a stand-alone decision-making tool that would not "disrupt existing financial systems" but would provide "realistic product costs, product design support, and an understanding of the cost of complexity while improving sourcing decisions"--- and proposed a three year schedule for implementing ABC at CPC's six remaining stamping plants and seven engine plants. The team also proposed formation of a CPC ABC Liaison Group that would be managed by the Plant Comptroller and would include a member from the ABC team and three system designers. Each implementation site was to designate three employees with production experience for their ABC Design Team. CPC's ABC Liaison Group would train the team and oversee implementation. An ABC team member remembered preparing for the meeting:

> We knew it wouldn't be an easy sell. There were competing ideas, mainly machine hours ... we developed counter-arguments about why we didn't think machine-hour costing would solve the problem. We also anticipated resistance that stemmed from 'not-invented-here' feelings among the corporate people. CPC accounting people had been working with the modernized plants to develop machine-hour systems... they were predisposed to that approach.

She also remembered concerns that were raised in the meeting:

> People hadn't heard of it [ABC] and didn't understand what the implications of changing the cost system might be... they thought it [the ABC model] was too complex, and it was. We knew that 78 cost drivers were too many. In response we started studying how much cost was driven by each cost driver and what the effect would be if we started eliminating cost drivers.

> The resources required to implement and maintain the system were another big sticking point: computers and manpower... management wanted to have a dollar benefit for implementing ABC.

The Director of Product Cost for CPC recalled the meeting:

> ...the results of the pilot showed disturbing differences between the ABC piece cost and the traditional piece cost... I would say that by the end of the meeting they were energized to move ahead with something that got us closer to the truth... I remember [GM's Comptroller] saying 'You're preaching to the choir, let's move ahead with it.' The team wanted to refine it [the ABC model]... but the momentum was there for corporate involvement to roll it out ...That evening after the meeting [the Director of Finance] asked me if I would take this group under the CPC product cost group...

Team members remembered the outcome of the meeting differently:

> We were pretty depressed... An important person in the meeting was visibly distracted during the presentation... we were hit with so many trivial objections. We were pretty certain that was the end of it, although we had permission to continue at our plant.

When questioned about the seemingly disparate beliefs about the future of ABC that emerged from the August 1987 meeting, the Director was surprised and replied that the team,

> ... should have been elated not depressed... in their presentation they lacked an overall cost management vision and were unable to address how to make it 'fit' with existing systems--- they were really undisciplined. One of our objections was that many of the inaccuracies that their system 'corrected' were driven by flaws in their traditional system not by improvements offered by ABC. A poorly executed labor-based system isn't a basis for accepting ABC...

Despite their pessimism, the team returned to the plant where they were joined by the GMR researchers to complete ABC implementation in the plant's second major production area. Three of the four original ABC team members departed and project leadership devolved to the remaining original team member, with the plant Comptroller continuing as the project sponsor. As CPC's Director of Product Cost predicted, seven months later these two people (hereafter referred to as the CPC ABC Sponsor and Designer) were relieved of their plant responsibilities and assigned to lead the ABC effort from CPC's Product Cost group. The March, 1988, transfer announcement stated:

> [the Comptroller] is going to head up the development and implementation of the ABC System for CPC, and the [existing ABC plants] will be the lead plants for this more effective processing.

Although they were officially CPC employees, they remained at the plant to complete the ABC model and manage the transition from implementation to maintenance. They continued to provide technical support to plants experimenting with ABC, developed a Design Manual documenting ABC implementation steps, and defined their jobs to include providing ABC design support, ABC training, and "user"[6] support.

Although creation of a CPC Group-level ABC team suggests that ABC was moving toward adoption, the ABC team leader described the atmosphere as:

> ...wait and see... CPC management was still asking 'what benefits are we actually going to get from it?' ... there was no official mandate to implement ABC... plants called us if they were interested and we were there to support them if they were willing to commit resources to it.

The ABC Sponsor was not authorized to hire additional ABC Designers as had been proposed. This is not to say that there was not CPC Group-level support for the effort. On the contrary, every person interviewed cited the support of CPC's Director of Finance from 1987 until his retirement in late 1992 as the impetus for moving the discussion of cost system innovations from the plants and Groups to the Corporate level. As one person remembered:

> His vision was an integrated system that would accurately define the cost of a vehicle...and future vehicles...he believed that it really helped you [if you could] predict the future ... 'If I can't afford the present, then I can't afford the future by continuing,' ... He had a vision of using better current information to project future product data...He was not trying to outsource a floor pan.

In sum, it would be premature to call formation of the two-person CPC ABC group a sign of ABC adoption. The team was physically isolated and had no authority to expand ABC's scope, although they had support at the top of the CPC organization. What can be concluded is that the influence of other cost experiments on the trajectory of the corporate cost system was sharply limited. As the Director of CPC Product Cost recalled,

> ...by then the [factored-piece time] approach was gathering dust on a shelf... I don't think it was considered practical. It was an interesting study and showed tremendous effort by a few people. But it was clear that if you wanted to replicate that you would have to... spend the same amount of energy at every location. It just wasn't something you would want to foist on others... ABC was the first thing we saw that had the discipline, took existing information, had a practical amount of input from experts--- manufacturing and production people--- and gave you the sense that we're really starting to ask people for their thinking about where our costs are coming from.

As part of GM's commitment to technological innovation, an external panel of world-renown scientists, called the GM Science Advisory Committee (SAC), periodically reviews company practices and advises top management. In Spring, 1988, the SAC was charged with reviewing GMR, and concluded in their final report that:

> A research group should be formed combining appropriate people from GMR and the central Finance and Accounting staffs and directed to study cost accounting problems.

In response, managers from GMR naturally recommended CPC's ABC approach as a model for corporate expansion. The two researchers who participated in the plant implementation, their supervisor, and CPC's ABC Sponsor met with GM's Vice-President of Finance in early summer and the outcome of the meeting was the formation, in October 1988, of the Cost Systems and Measurements Council (CSMC).

The CSMC was charged with reviewing and recommending changes to existing cost practices as well as developing a comprehensive performance measurement system to support advanced manufacturing methods. Three individuals jointly chaired the Council: the top managers of ACG and GMR, and GM's Assistant Comptroller. The Council was supported by a workgroup that was based in Pontiac and headed by the secretary of the CSMC, a member of the corporate finance staff. One of the GMR researchers, the CPC ABC Sponsor and the CPC ABC Designer were assigned to the cost team of the CSMC workgroup. The ABC Designer described the significance of the CSMC:

> The cost part of the CSMC [study] was translated as ABC... meaning that we were going to look at ABC and only ABC and we were not going to consider machine hour costing or anything else. Basically it was going to be ABC.[7] Though the decision continued to be an issue in the lower ranks, it was pretty much resolved in the minds of top management. Formation of the Council indicated a recognition that ABC had potential as a corporate-wide system. The CSMC workgroup's cost team was to evaluate this possibility.

The cost team of the CSMC workgroup was charged with assessing the feasibility of ABC as a corporate strategy. In the February, 1989, CSMC meeting, the team was given four guidelines for developing a corporate ABC proposal:

1) It must support engineers' assessment of alternative product designs;

2) It must have the potential for providing information at different levels of aggregation (e.g., plant level, division level, and vehicle level);

3) It should be comprehensive, covering implementation plans for all North American manufacturing operations; and,

4) The implementation strategy should address people issues, ensure that new information generated by the system is not threatening and suggest plans for facilitating the understanding of the data.[8]

The workgroup identified two prerequisites to ABC becoming a corporate strategy. First, they had to demonstrate that ABC was applicable to a variety of process settings, including vehicle assembly, machining, stamping, molding, specialty processing and component assembly. Although eleven plants had installed ABC systems, they did not cover the spectrum of processes. Second, they needed to link ABC to corporate strategies for improved performance and show that ABC data precipitated better decisions. Although the Pontiac pilot study demonstrated that ABC product costs were different from traditional product costs it did not provide examples of uses of ABC data.[9] To address these issues the team proposed in the April 1989, CSMC meeting to implement ABC at eleven additional sites and to develop case studies from all 22 sites that would focus on uses for ABC data in management decision-making. The Council approved the plan asking for a complete evaluation of ABC by February 1990.

In the following month, the cost team approached the eleven plants identified for the expanded ABC pilot study. Seven agreed to participate[10] and one unsolicited volunteer emerged, bringing the pilot sample to 19 plants that represented most GM production processes. The next step was linking the sites to tests of system usefulness:

> ... initial studies focused on differences between traditional product costs and ABC product costs. That was the main measure of system validity... the CSMC pilots expanded that to 'What kinds of decisions would you typically want to apply this better cost information to?' ...We figured out the claims that we wanted to make for ABC about decisions it supported ... we wanted to focus on sourcing, investment decisions, pricing, and continuous improvement.

> We presented the list to the plants and said 'Which of these make sense... Are these hot issues in your plant... things that the ABC pilot could help support?'... we tried to identify a natural match ... we asked them why they were doing ABC and how they wanted to use it... I think it was considerably less than universally true that they eagerly supported looking at decision support...

Three new members joined the CSMC cost team to assist in training and advising the pilot sites. The ABC training program was expanded to incorporate GM experiences and to focus on action plans and specific implementation steps:

> We gave them specific instructions based on learning from earlier implementations. We explained their role in the CSMC study and our time frame. After implementation the teams were to present their results to their management and to attempt to use ABC for specific decisions of the type they were assigned to investigate. Then they were to develop a business case using their data that we would present to the Council and use for future training.

Evidence that ABC might become corporate policy came on June 21, 1989, as GM Chairman and CEO, Roger Smith, spoke to the National Association of Accountants (now the Institute of Management Accountants) in Cincinnati, OH. He reported that GM recognized problems in cost accounting practices, had been studying ABC since 1986, and was piloting it in 19 sites in hopes of "... find[ing] out if it can help us improve our costing techniques."

In their September 1989 progress report, the cost workgroup defined thirteen implementation benchmarks and reported each site's progress on a Gantt chart. The workgroup monitored the plants' progress against three criteria:

> ...we looked at where they were in the design process--- had they identified activity centers and cost drivers ...we assessed whether they were trying to understand and do analysis of their existing costs versus the ABC costs--- if they were trying to understand why some costs changed... those reviews got people thinking about cost flows, activities, process changes, and really drove the organization to understand the concepts... These first two indicators were clear-cut...The third factor that we looked at was the qualitative side of implementation... based on our impression of the team's involvement, divisional management's involvement, how the data was used after it was developed and whether there was support for it at the site... When we developed our report for the Executive Council we evaluated what had driven qualitative differences... training, application of the concepts, or other factors.

Even in the pilot study, the cost workgroup observed mixed success in implementation. Believing that factors related to management support and communication were critical success factors, the team requested that the CSMC provide greater visibility to the pilot teams through frequent communications with group-level managers and management support for full-time staffing of the local ABC teams and formation of plant-level steering committees. Subsequent monthly CSMC meetings included testimonials by team members from successful implementations about how the data was being used and indicated that 18 of the pilots would meet the January deadline.[11]

In February 1990, the cost workgroup presented results from the 18 pilot sites that demonstrated that ABC data had the potential to support decision making in the five areas that were investigated and that revealed significant changes in product costs at most of the production sites. The Council assessed the pilot study's success using three criteria:

> One question was 'Can we even do this... does it have broad applicability [beyond stamping]?'... I think the answer to that was a fairly clear, 'Yes'...

> The second criteria [was]... does it make any difference? Is there any evidence that going through all this tells us anything different than the current accounting system? The answer again was a pretty clear, 'yes'...

The third aspect was 'How does this contribute to decision-making in the specific areas that we had chosen to look into?' ...the results of that were less clear-cut, largely because we hadn't worked out (and I'm still not sure we have worked out) exactly how to design one of these ABC systems so that it really supports decision-making...There wasn't overwhelming evidence from these pilots--- you couldn't add up how many dollars we saved as a result of implementing ABC---which [would have] made evaluation easy... I think the plants said 'OK, we'll crunch the numbers for you and when we're done you can do your analysis.' But I don't think they really warmed to the idea of reinventing the decision-making process for their plant.

Another workgroup member recalled the ensuing debate among Council members:

The main negative perception was that real-time decisions weren't made... [during the study] there wasn't a major outsourcing decision so the plants had to look at past decisions or had to extrapolate to some possible future decisions... There was a perception among Council members that this made the results weak. Another problem was that we couldn't present a dollar benefit to the Council for implementing ABC... Also, some of the plants' product costs didn't change very much... In most cases this was because they had used a lot of volume-based cost drivers in their models... some of it reflected intentional resistance and some was just misunderstanding the ABC theory... Of course we couldn't really say this since they were 'volunteers'... Politically it just wasn't the best way to handle it. Instead we assessed typical reasons for failure and included them in our training programs.

One concern that Council members raised in the meeting was the role of subjectivity--- identifying activities and selecting cost drivers--- in designing ABC systems. Before they would decide on the future of ABC, the Council directed the team to conduct a follow-up study comparing cost drivers used in two stamping plants to identify the degree to which subjective selection of cost drivers influenced product costs and to evaluate the potential for developing a common "cost driver list" to guide future ABC implementations. Other concerns included: a corporate rollout schedule; whether ABC should be a corporate or local initiative; which costs should be included in ABC models; how to communicate ABC to the larger GM community; how to integrate and reconcile ABC models with existing financial systems; and finally, the source of resources for implementing ABC.

In March, the team presented a comparative analysis of ABC systems in stamping environments and concluded that "a list of core cost drivers would be a useful starting point for implementation;" however, further analysis was required to identify the cost drivers. In an early indication of migration of the project's objectives from product to process costing, the team based its recommendation for adopting ABC on what they called "the primary benefit of supporting cost reduction" activities in a manner that considers "total organizational costs." They recommended that ABC be developed as a stand-alone, PC-based system because integration across diverse systems would pose too great a problem in the short-run. (However, in the long run, all financial systems were to be harmonized with ABC data.) Of the 18 pilot sites, nine intended to continue using ABC, five liked ABC but did not have the resources to support two cost systems, and four did not like ABC and would not continue to support it.[12] At the meeting's conclusion the CSMC endorsed ABC as the recommended approach and directed the team to complete a rollout plan and present their findings to the Executive Committee and to the CFO's Staff Meeting. In April the team proposed a five year rollout schedule for GM NAO. The Council amended this to three years, requesting completion by 1993.

In their last presentation to the CSMC in May 1990, the cost team proposed an organizational structure for supporting ABC that was accepted by the Council. An ABC Steering Committee, comprised of the four Groups' Directors of Finance, the Assistant Comptroller, the ABC Sponsor and the GMR researcher, would guide the ABC implementation effort. Each Group (e.g., CPC, BOC) would have a team of ABC liaisons to support the plants. One liaison would represent the Group on the ABC Oversight Committee, a working arm of the ABC Steering Committee that was headed by the ABC Sponsor.

In June 1990, the CSMC cost team presented evidence from the pilot study to the Executive Committee. One participant remembered:

... We talked through the concepts briefly... then we reviewed the results... we had pretty much complete buy-in all the way through. In fact [the CFO] said that the existing costs systems were inadequate--- 'not what we need to run the business.' He wholeheartedly supported moving forward with corporate implementation.

With this endorsement the meeting turned to issues of implementation. The Committee agreed to the proposed organizational structure; thus the cost team of the CSMC workgroup was renamed the ABC Steering Committee, and became the backbone of the new ABC Oversight Committee. The perennial concern of how ABC would fit with the corporate strategy of common systems (e.g., the integrated production scheduling and inventory control (PSIC) system) was raised and the Steering Committee was directed to pursue "common systems with different approaches" in the design of future ABC models. Corporate implementation was to be completed by 1993, with each Group determining a schedule of plant implementations to insure attainment of the goal. Thus, in June 1990, four years after the pilot study of transactions-based costing, management adopted ABC as GM corporate policy.

3. GENERAL MOTORS' DEPLOYMENT OF ABC

In the months preceding the first ABC Steering Committee meeting on November 16, 1990, the Groups devised plans for implementing ABC by 1993. As was the case in the CSMC pilot study, plants were selected "partly [through] volunteerism and partly based on the realities of knowing whether the plant was in turmoil ... not wanting to dump one more task on top of them." At the meeting, the Director of ACG laid out an aggressive schedule of implementing 41 plants in 1991, 38 in 1992 and 31 in 1993. CPC's Finance Director reported that their stamping plants were either completed or in progress. The modernized plants, where implementation had been postponed until completion of the CSMC pilot, were pioneering a new process aimed at "commonizing" key ABC design choices, such as major cost centers and cost drivers, for all CPC stamping plants. CPC was also building the first non-manufacturing ABC model to support cost analysis of die-building activities. The Truck and Bus Group reported that the pilot implementation at one of their two stamping plants had not been maintained; local ABC designers were reassigned to different jobs and there was no plan to update the model because plant management had "no use for the data." No plans for implementing ABC in the BOC Group or the newly formed GM Power Train Group (GMPT) were presented.

These presentations motivated discussion on three crucial issues that shaped the Steering Committee's agenda for several months thereafter. First, the managers were concerned that ABC was not being communicated as a corporate policy to plant management. Part of the problem was that ABC publicity had been directed to the accounting community. The group decided that future ABC memos should be directed toward operational rather than financial uses of ABC data and should be circulated to plant managers and others in the manufacturing community. They also decided to name GM's CFO as the official "Corporate ABC Champion" to heighten awareness of the ABC initiative. A second related issue was that in the absence of a strong endorsement of ABC, managers relied on traditional systems that were not easily reconciled to the ABC system. Thus, integrating ABC with existing financial and operating systems became an item for Steering Committee investigation. Finally, the apparent failure of the Truck and Bus implementation to inspire management support caused Steering Committee members to comment that ABC "needs to be restructured as a 'pull-system' " with top management requiring cost information to be derived from ABC data. The ABC Sponsor was asked to identify all uses of plant-level cost data at the Group level and to distinguish uses that could be satisfied by ABC data.

The ABC Steering Committee met quarterly and the Oversight Committee met monthly. The Oversight Committee's mission included training local designers, monitoring implementations, advising local teams on ABC design, providing software support, and serving as the hub of ABC communications. Training evolved from a focus on technical skills to a focus on strategic cost management skills:

> [in the] training sessions... [we found] it was better to focus on the broad concepts...to make sure people understood what the need for change was and how the system could provide better cost information and how that information could be used in a more strategic way...When people saw it simply as a product costing system... you didn't get the buy-in--- the non-financial people were not as interested and it made implementation harder.

Advising was limited to software support and application of the broad concepts of ABC:

> We tried to stay away from a 'cookbook approach'... we set guidelines and [said] 'here's how other teams have structured their process'... we tried to build entrepreneurial spirit and let the teams take ownership for their implementation. We didn't claim to be experts about individual plants; we tried to be experts in addressing system problems and conceptual problems... consultants rather than on-line implementers.

To increase ABC's visibility, the Oversight Committee employed three publicity vehicles. First, the minutes of all Committee meetings were circulated to the Groups' operating areas. Second, they approached the General Technical Council (a GM Board-level committee) and the Manufacturing Technical Council (an executive-level council) for endorsement:

> ...by presenting [to them] and getting their endorsement we became part of their minutes...we started ... putting on other shows within other subcommittees. So we were building awareness and ... We were trying to develop the customer-supplier relationship [for information]...

Finally, the ABC Sponsor was a tireless advocate for ABC:

> ...[the ABC Sponsor] was the chief implementer, agitator, salesman, educator of ABC... he spent most of his time making awareness presentations... He'd start with... a management awareness presentation to the general manager and his staff--- if you don't have support at that level, you're not likely to succeed...he was ready to travel to any unit ... He had such a long list of contacts---engineers, design types, GMR people--- he accomplished a lot through just a network of people who were interested in ABC. I don't think he got a lot of official help.

In addition to publicizing ABC within GM, the ABC Sponsor developed a national reputation by speaking at conferences, representing GM at Computer

Aided Manufacturing-- International (CAM-I), and teaching in an executive program at the University of Michigan's School of Business Administration. In mid-1990, his counterpart at Chrysler contacted him to discuss ABC in the first of what was to become an ongoing exchange about ABC implementation. The Chrysler manager recalled their first meeting:

...ABC at GM had gone much further than I had previously understood... not only had they done multiple plants, they had visions of doing the entire company... and they had a timetable and an action plan to get there...[he] had trained 600 people ...[He] also shared with us how difficult it was to get people interested and to understand the implications of a direct-labor based system... I walked away... knowing that these guys really have a jump on Chrysler on this one.

[After the meeting] we were able to communicate to management here... that GM appeared to be ahead of us on this initiative; that they had, from a product cost and strategic planning side found out that their product costs were significantly different under ABC; and it was leading to different decisions. One of the early challenges that kept coming up at Chrysler was 'Are people really doing something different?' and without any specifics we were told that GM was making different sourcing and investment decisions... That was important for people to know.

Thus GM became known in the business community as a leader in ABC implementation; a role that solidified internal support for ABC at the corporate level.

The March 1991, Steering Committee meeting was again focused on insuring that plans were in place to meet the 1993 deadline. ACG's Finance Director reported that the Group was moving ahead, but remarked that he was concerned about whether completed implementations were being updated as a result of severe resource constraints in the plants. ABC was still viewed as a "special study" and typically local designers returned to their original jobs after building the ABC model. He questioned whether central coordination of the expanding set of implementations was adequate and suggested that this failure may explain poor utilization of ABC data in cost analyses. On the heels of this remark, and in response to previous concerns about system integration, the Committee decided to seek closer ties to the Financial Systems Steering Committee, a corporate group that was evaluating ways to harmonize diverse systems in a single corporate control system.

CPC's Finance Director reported completion of ABC implementation in one modernized stamping plant and indicated that the common design approach had been successful. The CPC Group Liaison who led the commonization effort described the process:

[CPC's Director of Finance] wanted a common stamping model to be determined before extending ABC to the modern stamping environment...Management agreed that the stamping plants should commonize, but the people at the plant weren't committed to it. I summarized everyone's [non-modernized stamping plants] initial designs--- for example, everyone allocated utility dollars over machine hours--- and identified areas of disagreement. We called a meeting of all of the teams and [the ABC Sponsor] and I facilitated the discussion.

An Oversight Committee member described the commonization effort as an attempt to "put limits on" system differences that arise naturally from training programs that promoted entrepreneurial spirit and system ownership. During the CPC commonization meeting, disagreements arose concerning informational needs of individual plant managers and the level of detail required to support those demands. There were also disputes about the 'right' cost drivers for tracing specific costs to products.

"We had a mix of generations of implementations--- they had a lot of knowledge and experience. Later implementations had already benefited from [one plant's] experience, so it wasn't as if they had designed their systems independently. Then we had some plants that had just been trained. They weren't sure about what they were going to do---they obviously didn't know whether they should fight for something or not. The Truck and Bus plant [an invited guest to the otherwise CPC meeting] had a really unique design... there was a lot of ownership to that one and they did not want to give up much... we were trying to be conscious of not forcing the design on everyone ... The main criterion for settling disputes was balancing costs of getting information with benefits...If the information was available people were more willing to change."

Ultimately, the plants differed in the degree to which they used the common design. The CPC Liaison reviewed each model and negotiated with local team members if their design choices were believed to distort product costs or to represent a misapplication of ABC design principles.

The Director of CPC Finance reported a second innovation at the March Steering Committee meeting. CPC was taking the first step to reconcile ABC data with traditional financial systems and move ABC from the status of "special study" to an integral part of the financial control system by developing its 1992 budget based on ABC data where it was available. The biggest challenges were: linking the traditional concepts of fixed and variable costs to the ABC model; reconciling actual production volumes with budgeted production volumes; and, distinguishing costs that were included in the budget and in traditional product costing but which were not traced to products in the ABC system (e.g., future-product costs). An Oversight Team member recalled:

Other issues that came up that we tried to resolve from a Corporate standpoint [was]... integration with other system developments...we were developing common systems... common accounts receivable and common payable systems... everybody was trying to understand how ABC would fit in that environment... we need commonality among the other systems before we can commonize the cost system.

The Finance Director of Truck and Bus announced that ABC would be revived at the existing ABC site but that plans for implementing at the second plant were delayed pending resolution of workforce-related issues. The BOC Group Finance Director reported that BOC stamping plants would implement ABC in 1991. The GMPT Group Finance Director indicated that training was complete and implementation underway at nine sites; the remaining seven sites would be implemented after 1991.

The minutes of the first two meetings of the ABC Steering Committee hint at the early frustrations with ABC and the Groups' mixed resolve in the early stage of ABC adoption. They also highlight significant system and design process adaptations. When asked to comment on the relative enthusiasm of the Groups in embracing ABC and developing implementation plans, an Oversight Committee member said:

...CPC was the most aggressive, but they also had the most non-assembly plants. The ACG had about 75% of the job to get done and they ... were pretty aggressive in their timetable in moving out into at least one site per division. I'd say Truck & Bus and BOC probably were not as aggressive. I don't know that it was so much a factor that they didn't have the same problems as CPC did, but they clearly had more assembly plants and fewer component operations...they had bigger things on their agenda...Delco Electronics [reports through Hughes Aircraft and GM-Hughes Electronics and was represented on the Steering Committee though not officially part of the GM NAO ABC mandate] was probably up with the ACG as far as implementation.

While some Groups reluctantly accepted ABC, others rapidly adapted it to fit their information needs. Those who led the adaptation process shaped the ABC system that gradually became institutionalized through "commonization" as the corporate standard. Adaptation continued as the population of ABC sites grew and local design teams introduced innovations in the design or use of the ABC system. Summer 1991 marked a clear transition to corporate acceptance of ABC.

The clearest indication of corporate acceptance and the intent to routinize ABC was publication on July 26, 1991, of Comptroller's Circular Letter (CCL) No. 2860, entitled "Implementation and Utilization of Activity-based Costing." Which identified corporate requirements for the implementation, maintenance and use of ABC. It reflected the Steering Committee's effort to transform the corporate ABC approach to one of 'pulling' ABC data from the plants rather than 'pushing' the ABC system on the plants. The following passages from CCL 2860 indicate ABC acceptance:

As a result of the endorsement and recommendations of the General Technical Committee, Manufacturing Technical Council, Competitive Cost Council, and Cost Systems and Measurements Council, the Corporation has recognized Activity Based Costing as the required system for assignment of overhead costs to activities or products... ABC implementation will be completed as soon as is practical, with December 1993 as the target for completion... phased timing requires that early adopters utilize the ABC product and activity costs as they become available in all decisions where product or activity cost information is required.

The initial focus of existing ABC implementations has been on manufacturing overhead costs... Initial ABC studies in non-manufacturing functions are now, or will be underway to define the applications of ABC to activities outside of manufacturing (e.g., engineering or commercial).

Key application areas to utilize the ABC information are represented by manufacturing and engineering special studies... ABC will not always be the primary decision support system for these decisions, but will facilitate improved decision making by providing a common information base of product and activity costs on which to model these issues in other decision support systems... ABC will also be utilized as a measuring device at the plant level to track the progress and continuous improvement resulting from operating decisions by the comparison of updated activity and product costs with those of previous ABC models. ABC information will also be linked to the Performance Measurement and Feedback System... one of the primary applications for...ABC product and activity cost information is the financial evaluation of product lines, manufacturing processes and production inputs... Other financial applications that are required to utilize ABC as the information base, when available, include Capital Appropriation Requests, Product Program and Pricing Proposals. Budget and Business Plan development must utilize the insights gained from ABC implementations in establishing the level of resources required to support production and processing of budgeted volume of products. General guidelines in the financial use of ABC information can be summarized by the requirement to use ABC activity or product costs wherever similar traditional costs are currently utilized. In this way, we will be basing our decision making on the best available cost information." [Emphasis original]

An Oversight Committee member recalled that the letter was well received by plants because it provided the first "tangible evidence of corporate support" and signaled plants to dedicate resources to ABC.

Although CCL 2860 recommended widespread use of ABC data, GM's Comptroller recognized that system interfaces were necessary to make these recommendations operational. In January 1992 he formed the Common Costing Practices Committee, including members from accounting, the ABC group and systems support (GM-EDS), to study ways to standardize and harmonize existing cost management practices. The committee developed a modular system, called the "Simplified Component Costing System" (SCCS) that interfaced with the budgeting, inventory valuation and production scheduling systems and used ABC cost data as an input.

In the year following CCL 2860, ABC training sessions were offered quarterly. Implementations proceeded at a pace dictated by the ability of the relatively small team of Corporate and Group ABC Liaisons to support new project teams. Previous implementation sites were encouraged to update their ABC models to reflect 1992 budgeted costs and the minutes of the May 1992 Steering Committee meeting confirm that implementation and maintenance were occurring; however, the Finance Director of ACG expressed frustration at the slow pace. Of 114 sites, ACG had completed only 21 and was concerned that the 1993 deadline was unrealistic. He expressed hopes that a new, fast implementation process, called "blitz implementation"[13] that was piloted at the end of 1991 in an Australian plant (GM Holdens) and replicated in a Delco plant in January 1992, could be used to meet the deadline. A Delco Electronics representative reported that they had used ABC data to identify costs of business processes and were attempting to motivate the elimination of non-value added activities. The perennial concern about communicating ABC to non-finance areas of the company was raised when the ABC Sponsor pointed out that Chrysler's ABC efforts were being driven by the enthusiasm of their President, Robert Lutz, whose background was in manufacturing and engineering. He also reported a disturbing trend that was emerging as ABC costs became available: plants were hesitant to provide information from ABC (product costs or ABC model design structure) to one another "for fear of losing competitive advantage."

These factors, in conjunction with growing awareness that improved product costs were not sufficient motivation for implementing ABC at some plants, caused the corporate ABC team to re-orient the ABC initiative during late 1992 and 1993. Moving away from the language of product costs, the group began to focus on activity or process costs as the key objective of the ABC system. Adopting the popular language of business process improvement, the team began to advertise ABC as a means for informing process re-engineering efforts, or "activity based management." The ABC software was modified to permit designers to classify costs (e.g., value and non-value added, and cost of quality categories such as prevention, appraisal and failure) in order to support detailed analysis of activity costs. While this increased the appeal of ABC at new implementation sites, it was difficult to change the perception of managers from earlier implementations that ABC was a product costing system. The result was reluctance on the part of these managers to commit plant resources to updating and maintaining the ABC model from year to year. The multi-disciplinary design teams disbanded and the maintenance task devolved to cost accountants in the plant.

In February 1993, GM assembled the first conference of ABC "users" representing every Group and most of the plants that had implemented ABC. The objectives of the meeting included: sharing design techniques; discussing software issues; identifying "implementation roadblocks" and discussing solutions; sharing success stories; and, establishing a network of ABC users in GM. The participants numbered over 100 and their responses to a survey conducted by the NAO ABC group indicated widespread enthusiasm for additional meetings. ABC implementers felt isolated at their plants and were encouraged to learn that others were facing similar challenges. The group met again in September 1993 with an even larger attendance. The substance of the meeting was similar[14], with each Group Liaison reporting their progress in implementing ABC. The evidence suggested that all NAO plants would be completed by early 1994.

By November 1993, it appeared that the deadline for complete ABC implementation in NAO would be met, with over 150 different ABC models in existence.[15] Although all the ABC models were not adequately maintained and updated--- few plants had conducted a full activity analysis since the initial implementation, most simply revised the pool of costs to be allocated to correspond to the new year and added or deleted products as necessary--- every plant had an ABC model for some period between 1989 and 1993. One concern, raised by a Group Liaison, was that some recalcitrant plants had postponed implementation until the last possible moment and had scheduled 'blitz' implementations in the last quarter of 1993. Nonetheless, the minimal level of use necessary to support survival of the technology was attained by the close of 1993.

4. CHRYSLER'S ADOPTION OF ABC

Chrysler's ABC Program can be traced to the formation in early 1989 of the Product Financial Analysis (PFA) Group in the Finance area. PFA was formed to address a growing concern among top managers that the firm did not know the profitability of individual product lines. There was a sense that different "keepers of the numbers" provided different answers to the question of vehicle profitability. PFA formed to bring consistency and integrity to the process. The major problem that PFA members faced was forcing an accounting system that was designed to reports costs of functional areas to address the question of vehicle profitability. The manager of PFA recalled being surprised by the way that large overhead costs were arbitrarily spread over all vehicles. Surprise quickly turned to frustration when he was required to justify the reported product costs to representatives from engineering and marketing charged with improving vehicle profitability.

Coincidentally, the manager of PFA read Roger Smith's June, 1989 address to the National Association of Accountants in which he described General Motors' experimentation with activity based costing as a means of better understanding product costs. Following this lead, he began a comprehensive investigation of ABC that led him to consulting firms and to other Fortune 100 firms that were implementing ABC. Independent confirmation of his intuition arrived when in October 1989 a major supplier, U.S. Steel, approached the PFA group to discuss activity based costing at Chrysler. The steel manufacturer was exposed to ABC through collaborations with Northwestern University and the American Iron and Steel Institute. The steel manufacturer was concerned that traditional cost systems would cause its customers to adopt aluminum inappropriately in future car parts. U.S. Steel believed that if its customers adopted ABC, the visibility of all costs of ownership of steel versus aluminum would favor using steel in new parts.

The PFA group agreed to participate in AISI's study of the relevance of ABC in metal stamping operations and provided cost data from one stamping plant to researchers. By March of 1990 the study provided some evidence that Chrysler's traditional cost system suffered from distortions in product costs that ABC was intended to address. Arguing that PFA could not fulfill its mission using data from the traditional cost system and armed with evidence that major companies had reached similar conclusions and were using ABC to address the problem, in March 1990 the head of PFA delivered to the Group Controller of Product Development a proposal to launch a pilot study of ABC. The proposal suggested using a cross-functional team of local plant employees, guided by an outside consultant "to benefit from the mistakes of others." The stamping plant that had been used in the AISI study was suggested for study.

Permission was granted, and in June a major consulting firm presented plans for a pilot study. A task force reviewed the proposal and concluded that Chrysler could complete the study without outside assistance. The team agreed that ABC was likely to offer many benefits, including better sourcing decisions, better vehicle profitability data, an understanding of the cost drivers of the business and avenues for cost reduction. However, they believed that a team of five to seven Chrysler employees with skills in budgeting, product costing, finance, vehicle costing and industrial engineering could develop simple ABC models for three plants with the cooperation of local managers.

Fortunately, before launching this pilot study, the task force visited several firms that were experienced in ABC implementation, including General Motors. Several insights emerged from these benchmarking studies. All of the firms warned that building a simple, partial ABC model without direct involvement of local managers was unlikely to provide a real test of the usefulness of ABC. The team was advised to limit the scope of the pilot study by selecting smaller locations that nonetheless exhibited product and process complexity, but to develop full models that included all costs. They were also advised to use local employees to insure that the ABC model captured relevant complexity and to augment the team with corporate resources to insure that the ABC theory was properly implemented. A prescient insight that was captured in a memo summarizing the results of the task force's visits was that "ABC is not an accounting system. It is an operational system. Better product cost data is a downstream, secondary benefit...ABC is a competitive weapon because it focuses on improvement opportunities... as a result ABC implementation at Chrysler should be led by operating personnel and supported by finance (and possibly a consultant)." Another insight that later proved false was, "ABC is not a long term system implementation. It can be installed in a relatively short period of time and can be run on a personal computer... this is not a "tear-up" of existing systems. It can be done quickly and at reasonable cost. GM reports using about 3000 man hours for each implementation."

Based on what was learned in these visits, the task force pulled back from its earlier recommendation and in November declared the "research" phase completed. They proposed that they be allowed to present their research to senior management and requested permission to conduct a single, full implementation of ABC at the stamping plant used in the AISI study using local employees under the guidance of an external consultant. Subsequently, after developing criteria for a good pilot implementation site the task force selected another stamping plant for study. It was felt that a stamping plant was a sufficiently complex setting for proving the value of the ABC technology and the particular plant selected was viewed as having a receptive plant manager and good union relations. The latter criteria was considered important for insuring that an accurate model could be developed with little overt resistance and for promoting use of the ABC data after the model was completed.

During 1990, while the PFA group was researching ABC, an unrelated quality management initiative was being implemented in operations management. Robert Lutz, President of Chrysler, had made total quality management and continuous improvement the theme of his administration. He personally visited companies that were known for product quality and with the assistance of his Vice President of Quality, brought the Crosby quality program to Chrysler. In the course of these benchmarking efforts, Lutz noted a recurrent theme of managing the quality of "business processes." He became a proponent of process management and one example of the implications of this new thinking was the reorganization of Chrysler's product development staff around product "platforms" --- cross-functional teams that were intended to work on a product program from initial design through product launch and manufacture. Not long thereafter, the VP of Quality encountered ABC at one of the companies where he was benchmarking quality management methods. He was intrigued by ABC because he had experienced firsthand the hindrance that financial systems posed to process management as a result of a focus on functional areas. Upon returning to Chrysler he became very outspoken about failures of the Finance group to support the quality initiative, specifically citing the fact that they "knew nothing" about ABC as evidence of the degree to which they were out of step with top management's goals.

The Vice President of Quality's criticism was just the catalyst that the task force needed to force the transition from investigation of ABC to experimentation with it. The task force reviewed its proposal with Chrysler's Controller and the Vice-President of Quality in December 1990. The VP of Quality was surprised and pleased to learn that ABC was under investigation and asked the team to prepare a detailed proposal for a pilot study. At the start of 1991 as the Gulf War escalated, Chrysler's top managers froze all discretionary spending. After reviewing the task force proposal in April, the Controller agreed that the conceptual basis of ABC was sound and warranted testing. Commenting on her conversation with the Controller in a memo to the task force, one finance manager noted that an independent study of internal management control practices had recently recommended modification or elimination of the traditional budget performance system. One criticism of the budget performance system was its dependence on fixed and variable cost distinctions. In the opinion of the finance manager, ABC, with its richer categories of the cost hierarchy, was a natural replacement for the system. In spite of strong support for the idea of ABC, spending constraints caused the Controller to insist that a formal request for proposal (RFP) be written to solicit bids from several consultants for the pilot study. Between April and September, an ABC Steering Committee was formed and began to contact leading consulting companies.

In September 1991, four consulting firms' proposals were formally reviewed. Among the four firms that presented plans for a pilot study and a subsequent corporate rollout, fees for the pilot study ranged from $150K to $450K with estimated times to completion of 16 to 22 weeks. Estimated prices for the corporate program ranged from $2.3M to $8.7M with lower priced bidders promising a two-year completion and higher priced bidders claiming that completion time would be determined after the firm provided more details about the engagement. Criteria used to evaluate the proposals were:

- Whether the firm evinced a philosophy of ABC that went beyond product costing and recognized ABC as an integral information system for supporting operations
- Experience of the firm in implementing ABC in multi-site, multi-product settings where all costs are to be fully allocated, as evidenced by long-standing working systems.
- Experience of the firm's current employees in complex ABC implementations, in particular in the metal stamping setting.

- Proposed ABC software, its features and capability, maturity, and likelihood of ongoing support and enhancements.[16]
- Evidence that the firm understood the "people side" of ABC implementation. One firm was singled out as the only one to recognize that the ABC interview process (used to define business activities and to identify appropriate cost drivers) would be threatening to plant employees and warranted careful consideration in the planning process.
- Ability to provide training programs in support of the implementation.
- Ability to complete the job in a timely manner and willingness to cost all products and assign all costs to products (e.g., no partial studies).[17]
- Quality and type of previous relationships with Chrysler, likelihood of "fitting in" at local plants, and whether it seemed likely that they would be responsive to plant staff concerns.

In October 1991 a consultant was selected and the Controller sent a memo to Chrysler's President, Robert Lutz, notifying him of the start of a pilot study of ABC. In his words, "We believe that ABC is an innovative and exciting tool that will allow finance staffs to support corporate competitive advantage." Interestingly, another memo sent to senior managers from the head of PFA appears to have been aimed at galvanizing the organization into action using GM's progress in implementing ABC as a prod. The memo claimed that at GM, ABC implementation is driven by plant-level personnel with virtually no involvement of corporate staff and that GM believes this approach is critical to creating ownership at the plant level for the ABC system. The memo also reports that GM had implemented ABC in over 40 locations, had trained approximately 600 people, anticipated completion of implementation by 1993 and was actively rolling out ABC to international operations and non-manufacturing operations.

The pilot study was launched with a series of meetings designed to explain ABC to the local management and prepare the organization for the implementation project. A major thrust of the meetings was learning about local management problems. The objective was to design an ABC system that would shed light on existing issues. With the launch of the pilot study, the steering committee, which had little involvement in the development of the ABC model, considered launching a smaller pilot study in a staff function. Consistent with PFA's mission of determining vehicle profitability, committee members believed that it was necessary to demonstrate that ABC could be applied to the corporate overhead costs that had previously been assigned to products in an arbitrary manner. The proposal was tabled when a survey of group controllers revealed mixed support for starting another study before completion of the stamping plant pilot study.

In the mean time, the pilot study moved through a succession of model development steps, including:

October 1991: Conducted interviews to define key business processes and began training for over 200 salaried managers and union representatives.

November 1991: Finalized the activity dictionary, which represented the full range of activities that would be included in the ABC model, and distributed "Work Distribution Forms", which were surveys designed to elicit how employees divided their time among these activities. Work distribution surveys for over 1500 employees were coded by the end of the month.

December 1991: Selection of first stage cost drivers begins. Few of the cost drivers are available in other information systems and the manual data collection causes concern among those who anticipate the difficulty of maintaining the system.

January 1992: Collection of data for first stage cost drivers is complete and second stage cost driver data collection is underway.

February 1992: preliminary data emerges from the system and the design team begins to hold meetings with local managers to present results.

The steering committee became involved in technical issues that would affect the evaluation of ABC as a corporate program, such as whether the costs included in the ABC model should be those from the current budget or the previous year actual costs, and what activities should be included in the activity dictionary. Otherwise the work of model design fell to the consultants and to two employees at the plant who were assigned full time to the task --- one budget supervisor and one hourly worker from the tool and die shop who had exceptional knowledge of the organization and considerable computing skills.

In December 1991 a change in senior management brought a new Controller. In meetings with Robert Lutz and the VP of Quality, the new Controller was told that Finance was moving too slowly in ABC implementation --- that they were "testing it to death." As the head of PFA recalled,

Bob Lutz believed in his heart that process management was the right way to go and he was saying 'I have to map my processes, I have to cost my processes and then I have to redesign them and make them efficient' --- and ABC was the cost part of the equation. ABC was the way that the Controller's Office would support continuous improvement.

By January 1992 it was generally acknowledged that ABC had succeeded in the pilot study. Reactions from local managers indicated that the ABC data were bringing new issues to the table. One local manager noted that "we are getting information that we did not have... we had a gut feel, but could not quantify the information. We recognize that we have significant work ahead of us and this will provide the basis for sound decisions and communication." Another manager's response was quite spontaneous: "I looked at this data and asked, 'why, why, why?' I was surprised by the level of supervision, waiting costs and unscheduled maintenance. We are reactive, not proactive...Safety, training, quality and planning activities are at the bottom of the list [lowest cost] This is a valuable tool as a stimulant to asking the right questions." However, their enthusiasm was tempered by a concern that ABC might not survive the departure of the consultants: "I am concerned about how we are structured to support ABC. We think you need a full time person to run ABC and [the consultant] should not leave until that person is in place."

In a January memo to Robert Lutz, the new corporate Controller stated that the pilot study, which would be completed in March, was progressing well and that preliminary results were providing new insights to manufacturing operations. Based on the success of the pilot study, he proposed initiation of a second phase of "ABC rollout" aimed at "establishing the ability to quickly rollout ABC to the remainder of the company in Phase III. Permission was granted and in early February the Controller signed a letter of agreement for consulting services associated with ABC implementation at eight new sites. The new sites included all remaining stamping plants (3), a parts plant, an engine plant, two service parts depots and one staff function. In addition, the consultant was charged with staying at the first ABC implementation site to "develop improved performance measures and support the internalization of the new ABC information" through application of the data to local problems. The consultant was also to provide guidance to a corporate ABC group that would begin to study comparisons of ABC data from common sites (e.g., the four stamping plants), to develop corporate training programs and to contemplate integrating ABC data into existing financial systems and decision processes. At the same time that the second wave of implementation projects was authorized, Chrysler adopted a more formal organizational structure to provide corporate support to the program. The head of PFA was placed at the head of a new group, called Activity Based Costing that included two staff members and several consultants.

In May 1992, top management got its first detailed look at ABC data from the pilot study. In a four hour officer's meeting that included Robert Lutz, Robert Eaton (Chairman, who had joined the company only weeks before), the Chief Financial Officer and all of the operational vice presidents, the consulting firm led a brief session on ABC concepts followed by the managers of the stamping plant presenting results of the ABC study. The head of PFA describes the meeting:

> That meeting was a major milestone …getting all of the officers of the company into one room for four hours to discuss financial systems was previously unheard of --- the officers got together for strategic planning, but not for something like this… Up until that time all I could show people was case studies from other companies. I always got the reaction, 'Well, that's not us, we're different, how do you know it's going to apply here? Now I had Chrysler data that showed it did apply here… The plant management team believes the numbers and is standing there in front of the room owning them --- so it took away a whole string of arguments that people used to have against ABC…
>
> Of course the plant staff was pretty nervous about standing up in front of the top managers of the company and showing data about operating inefficiencies. We met with Bob Eaton right before the meeting to tell him how important it was that everyone understood how threatening this information was and how nervous the plant staff was…Eaton did a great job of trying to set the record straight. He gave a great speech that we still call 'the wart speech.' He said that it was very positive for [the plant] to come forth and show its warts; that he felt that ABC was a tool to tell us where we are today; but his interest is not in doing a deep dive to understand how we got to where we are. His interest is, 'Now that we have this baseline information, where are you going and what is your rate of travel? What are your plans?' …He made it clear that as we implement ABC and uncover inefficiencies, this was not going to become a tool, like an operational audit, to embarrass people. His speech played a big role in the meeting in setting the tone.
>
> There were a lot of statements made by senior officers that clearly indicated that they supported the project … so the meeting was a major milestone and a major launching point for us because it was clear that this was starting to become a mandate … it became clear that there was going to be no turning back. Up until then there was still a lot of doubt as to whether Chrysler was really serious about this and whether some of the groups that opposed ABC could eventually unwind it. If one of our supporters changed positions or left the company, would ABC unravel? This was the first time when I said, 'we have senior management commitment.'

Thus, May 1992 marked the formal adoption of ABC by Chrysler as a corporate initiative. In 1993, asked to reflect on things that he would have done differently during the pilot study, the head of PFA pointed to the selection of the right pilot site as critical.

If I had to do it again I would have been a lot more careful. We focused on the plant, what it made and its cost structure. Today I would focus on the plant management team, the controller and the whole environment. Your pilot project is your most important one because when you start doing other plants, the very first reaction is 'I want to go to the first plant and see what they are doing with it.' I would also have defined success --- which we didn't do then. So we would have been able to say when we're done how would you describe success? How would you measure that? How would you know if you're there? Then, once I had defined success, I would have said, 'Which location would give me a higher probability of meeting that definition of success?'

Collaborations between the new Controller, the President and the Vice President of Quality in December 1991 indicated that ABC was part of their strategic vision for the company long before the pilot site was completed. However, although he was pleased to have strong top management support, in hindsight the head of PFA thought that a more linear process of evaluating the pilot study and using it to structure subsequent implementation could have provided early indications of organizational problems that came to light the following year. Although the pilot study was completed in the 12-20 weeks originally planned, it was clear in hindsight that the consulting firm poured extra resources into the plant to insure success of the pilot study. The head of PFA noted, "We've never in any subsequent implementation made the original timetable --- a pretty good indication that the consulting firms who originally bid the job had no idea of what they were up against with an organization of this size and complexity."

5. CHRYSLER'S DEPLOYMENT OF ABC

In Spring 1992 "Phase II" of ABC implementation was launched. The plan was to repeat the procedures of the pilot study, using approximately the same complement of consultants and local employees at each plant. The ABC Group of Corporate Finance grew from two to twelve employees over the next six months and most new employees joined a plant ABC design team as part of their training in ABC.

Coincident to his participation in an education program at the Massachusetts Institute of Technology, the head of ABC was approached by a faculty member from the Sloan School who was interested in ABC. The faculty member asked to interview employees at the pilot site as well as at many of the newly launched Phase II sites. The head of ABC recalled the request and the reactions it precipitated:

When I was at MIT I talked at some length about our progress implementing ABC. I think [the faculty member] was skeptical about my claims about how smoothly it was going. He had concerns that we weren't doing training properly and that we weren't communicating with the site. We were going in, in typical consulting mode, doing a slide show, walking away from the meetings thinking that people understood what we were proposing. We had no idea of the organizational turbulence that existed... We wanted to let him interview the employees --- we weren't afraid to face the facts. We wanted to know if things weren't going well. Interestingly, the consultants were very threatened by this...they had created this whole perception that everything was going according to the master plan...But we were starting a transition at this point --- my staff and I were starting to feel a lot more comfortable about how to do this, what the issues were and what some of the problems were. So we decided to just tell the consultants that this is the way it's going to be. We are the client and we will start making a lot of decisions going forward.

[The faculty member] went to the plants and asked really basic questions, like "Why do you think Chrysler is implementing ABC?" or, "How are you going to use this information?" The responses were startling. People didn't understand what we were doing, why we were doing it or what it had to do with them and their job. His interviews also opened our eyes about the significant concern in the organization about how the data would be used...people were participating on blind trust, but they were confused and often scared.

By the time that this study was completed, the Phase II implementations were complete. Nonetheless, the ABC Group had failed its process check and intended to respond to the issues. In Fall 1992 another phase of plant implementations was launched with an entirely new approach aimed at addressing several concerns.

Between the second and third wave of implementations, the key insight was understanding how important local management commitment and the site implementation team was...In the second phase we rushed in quickly --- in many cases the site management team was told 'you're doing this' by a higher level person. Some of this came out of our May officer's meeting. Someone got real excited and rushed out of the meeting saying, 'Do this at site XYZ.' The next thing you know, the manager at the site got a call and two weeks later the consultants would show up and launch the project --- and the manager never thought there was anything wrong with what he had in some cases! Another thing was, we'd walk into the plant and say that we needed two full time people and after they caught their breath we'd tell them the type of people we needed...Eventually they'd give us some people, but often half way through we'd learn that it wasn't the best choice of people. There was a certain skill set, a certain personality, and a certain level of respect in the organization that the person needed to have...We found that the people we were given were people who were available --- and they were available for a good reason!

To counter these problems, the program was slowed substantially. The ABC team began conducting screening interviews and reviewing resumes of all employees who volunteered for the assignment. Desirable expertise and characteristics included knowledge of operations, knowledge of existing information systems, computer skills, evidence of being well regarded in the organization and evidence of being able to work unsupervised. Realizing his Group was comprised of finance specialists who lacked many of the skills to manage organizational issues, the head of ABC enlisted support from the MIT faculty member to conduct training clinics for his staff. A major focus of the clinics was defining the objectives of the group and reviewing the business processes that were intended to support attainment of the goals.

[These conversations] caused us to focus on why we were doing ABC...Is our goal better product costs? Is it to focus on operational issues? The more we talked about it we stared to realize that we'd been spending a lot of time trying to learn the technical aspects of ABC and to build correct ABC models that had the right number of activity centers and cost drivers...we were ignoring the fact that people didn't understand it. We concluded that the project was not sustainable because people were just going through this because it was the politically correct thing to do. We had to sit back and say, 'How can we change our roles to get people more involved, more excited... and basically insure that we would reach successful implementation consistently. We wanted to reduce the variability --- we couldn't even take credit for the sites in our second and third round of implementations that were successful.

This realization caused the group to rethink how they entered a prospective ABC site. First, managers of prospective sites were to be notified several months before implementation launch and given the opportunity to decline to participate in that round of implementations. If a manager agreed to consider implementation, the team conducted an initial visit aimed at getting to know the management team, discussing pressing issues in the facility and briefly review some of the benefits of ABC. A second visit, which occurred several weeks later, included interview with a cross-section of employees. The objective was to get a more detailed view of operating concerns. If the managers agreed to proceed, an executive training session was offered to explain ABC in greater detail and interviews of prospect ABC implementers followed. Managers received several interim briefings during the course of model design. A "mid-stream" review would occur after the ABC model was completed. The title, "midstream review" reflected the desire that this meeting was intended to raise questions about operating efficiencies that would lead to additional analysis and presentations of recommended action plans.

One problem with the new strategy's slower pace of implementation is that it threw up for question the wisdom of discontinuing the traditional costing system upon completion of an ABC model --- a strategy that the senior management insisted on from the start:

> We got into integration much earlier than GM…When I say 'integration', we wanted to get the ABC information into our product cost system, which affects systems that are used for strategic decisions…[GM's] strategy was to implement the entire company on a standalone basis and then, when North American operations was completely implemented they planned to do integration. We had manpower problems. So when we went into a plant and said, 'You have to do ABC and maintain it as a separate system in addition to doing everything you do today,' we experienced resistance…We were also concerned about having a second set of numbers and people arguing about numbers…So our Controller was insistent on integration…We decided that we would switch people to ABC [and turn off the old cost system] as they implemented it. They would then do ABC-based budgets and the beginning of the next model year their data would go into the product cost study based on ABC…We realize that we're going to have a mishmash, with some plants on traditional labor-based overhead and some plants on ABC--- but the alternative wasn't attractive. We were concerned that we were going to make too many bad decisions … when in fact the data is sitting there waiting to be integrated. (Head of ABC Group)

Chrysler's Controller summarized the problem that he faced in Fall 1993:

> My challenge is implementing ABC as rapidly as senior management wants it. They are convinced it is the way to go. My challenge is going slow enough to insure local results while keeping management satisfied that I'm going fast enough.

The new entry strategy was aimed at helping local managers understand what ABC was and how it could be useful in managing their operations. In an effort to address the large question, "Why Chrysler was adopting ABC" the ABC Group taped several speeches by top executives that answered this question. Answers to this question, which were presented in the executive overview and in the midstream review, are a good place to conclude the discussion of deployment of ABC in Chrysler:

> Chrysler is reinventing it's financial system…In the late 1920's Chrysler broke into a new market segment with the Desoto…It was around that time that many of our cost systems took root…. The world has changed

significantly since the early 1900's --- the Desoto is long gone but we still have the cost systems...Another problem with today's financial system is the focus on gathering numbers for the purpose of reporting to the outside world...ABC will provide a better understanding of which processes, products and customers are causing costs to happen. ABC is a process tool. It starts from the assumption that we all make choices. These choices generate activities that consume resources and resources cost money which can be tracked to cars and trucks.... My fellow officers and I have seen the results from ABC sites ...We would like to have ABC throughout the company as quickly as possible; however, we have to be patient --- We can't take a system that was put in place over 70 years ago and reinvent it without ensuring that it will work right... ABC will provide a central information system to guide Chrysler...I fully support the implementation of activity-based costing." [CFO, "ABC101" video transcript]

We can't begin a discussion of ABC without first understanding its complete interrelationship with and interdependence on our other quality and cost initiatives...Process redesign takes a look at process on a cross-functional basis and not only identifies process conformity, but asks, "is this process ...the right process?"...ABC will identify all of the true costs as you look through the value chain --- not just a formula allocation of costs in one functional area... ABC is nothing less than the road map to that success. By looking at the whole stream of cost in various activities, ABC permits overall cost optimization throughout the corporation...ABC will provide Chrysler with better, more accurate, more detailed information than has exited in the past. As a result, strategic and operational decision-making will be greatly enhanced...we'll have a truer answer to strategic questions such as "How much money do we make on each of our lines of vehicles?"...As I hope you can tell by now, I am extremely excited about activity based costing. I am a whole-hearted proponent of the continuous improvement advantages that ABC can provide and I want your active participation in implementing it throughout Chrysler." [President, *ABC101* video transcript]

6. A MODEL OF ABC IMPLEMENTATION

What do we learn from the history of ABC implementation at General Motors and Chrysler? Are the processes of implementation idiosyncratic to each firm or are there common themes that are consistent with what we know about implementing management innovations? We believe that the experiences of both firms in implementing ABC bears strong resemblance to experiences that other firms have had in implementing information technologies and that the research literature on managing organizational change provides accurate descriptions of the processes associated with these managerial innovations.

6.1 Studies of IT Implementation

Research on the implementation of information technology (IT) implementation has evolved in several stages. Early studies concluded that success was either "technologically determined" or "organizationally determined" --- that success was completely dependent on either factors related to the technology or on factors related to the culture of the organization.[18] These studies shared a rational view of IT implementation that ignored disruptions to familiar work practices, decision-making processes, and power relationships that commonly accompany IT implementation. Later studies found that IT failure was neither technologically nor organizationally determined, but rather, emerged from the complex interaction of social and technical factors (Trist and Bamforth 1951) that were critical in enacting organizational change.[19] More recently, researchers have argued that these theories are inadequate because they exclude many stakeholders' to the new IT system. Decision-making processes that use data from IT systems also require radical revision for benefits of the new system to be realized.[20] In this setting, successful implementation of new systems hinges on the organization's ability to accept potentially disruptive changes; changes that often shift the locus of knowledge and decision-making from one political faction to another.[21]

In a comprehensive review of empirical research studies, Kwon and Zmud (1989) describe the IT implementation literature as evolving from a "factors" model, in which researchers focused on factors that influence IT implementation success, to a "process" model, in which researchers shifted from a linear to an interactive model of IT development that incorporated perspectives of multiple stakeholders. They develop a model of IT implementation in which success negotiating six stages of implementation is influenced by five types of contextual factors. Lewin's (1952) three-stage model of organizational change (unfreezing, change, and re-freezing) is linked to traditional criteria of IT implementation success (acceptance and usage), to model the implementation process as six sequential (at times overlapping) stages: [22]

- initiation
- adoption
- adaptation
- acceptance
- routinization
- infusion

During initiation, pressure to change arises from internal needs or external competitive threats and a search for solutions begins. Adoption encompasses the selection of a proposed solution and the decision to invest resources to facilitate change. Adaptation follows as, in the process of changing, unforeseen needs or system shortcomings are identified. Acceptance reflects the minimal level of use and maintenance that the new technology requires to be sustained. Routinization is signaled by the complete replacement of old work practices by the new system; the IT application becomes a part of normal activities. Infusion arises when the IT application is used, often in unanticipated ways, to improve work effectiveness and is seamlessly integrated with other organizational systems (Cooper and Zmud 1990).

Kwon and Zmud identify five major contextual factors, each comprised of minor factors, which influence successful transitions between stages of implementation:

- characteristics of individuals associated with implementation
- organizational factors
- technological factors
- the task to which the technology is applied
- environmental factors

Important characteristics of individuals associate with implementation include: disposition toward change; education; job tenure; and, role involvement with the IT solution. Organizational factors shown to influence implementation are: the degree of centralized of decision-making; the degree of functional specialization; and, the existence of informal communication networks. Technological factors such as: complexity experienced by users; its compatibility with existing organizational structures and systems; and, the technical improvement relative to existing practices, are also determinants of implementation success. Important task characteristics include: task uncertainty; task variety; and, worker autonomy and responsibility. Important environmental factors are: heterogeneity of external demands on the organization; the uncertainty caused by external turbulence; and external communication networks.

We use strong parallels to the IT literature in the early studies of ABC described in Chapter 2. Kwon and Zmud reviewed prior research studies, mapped the key factors studied onto the six stages of implementation, and concluded that most research studies concentrate on too few contextual factors and too narrow a time frame of implementation. Failure to comprehend the full process and the key factors behind implementation promoted an incomplete, often conflicting account of IT implementation projects. See Figure 3.1.

***Figure 3.1*. A Factor-Stage Model of Information Technology Implementation**

Six Stages of Implementation:

Initiation → Adoption → Adaptation → Acceptance → Routinization → Infusion

Five Contextual Factors that Influence Success at Each Stage of Implementation:

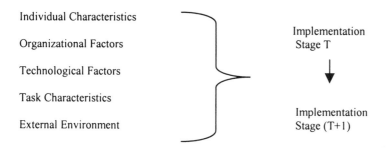

Individual Characteristics

Organizational Factors

Technological Factors

Task Characteristics

External Environment

Implementation Stage T

↓

Implementation Stage (T+1)

Adapted from Kwon and Zmud (19870 and Cooper and Zmud (1990)

When we reflect on the complex history of ABC implementation at GM and Chrysler and compare these rich accounts to the research literature on ABC discussed in Chapter 2, we have a similar concern. In Table 3.1 we tabulate the factors that Kwon and Zmud identified as compared to factors that have been suggested in both the research and practitioner literatures on ABC implementation.

Considering the path to corporate acceptance of ABC at GM and Chrysler, we were struck by the "epochs" of implementation progress at each firm, and have deliberately used Kwon and Zmud's language of staged implementation in our historical accounts. Using the corporate history of GM, Anderson (1995) theorized that different contextual factors are salient at different stages of implementation. Table 3.2 illustrates, using the GM case, how key contextual factors appear to be positively (+) or negatively (-) influential in the four stages of implementation that lead to acceptance of ABC as a corporate practice. We see similar patterns in the case history at Chrysler; however, a unique feature that accrues to "late adopters" of new

Table 3.1. **Candidate Variables for Exploratory Analysis of Factors Influencing Activity Based Costing Implementation Success by Literature Source**

CANDIDATE VARIABLE	IT Implementation Literature (Kwon & Zmud 1987)	Cost System Change Literature	Anecdotal Evidence from ABC Implementations
Individual Characteristics			
Disposition toward change/ Intrinsic reward in change	X	X	
Education	X		
Job Tenure	X		
Role Involvement	X	X	X
Informal support (e.g., sponsors, champions)			X
Organizational Factors			
Centralization	X		
Functional specialization versus Multi disciplinary approaches	X		X
Internal communications	X	X	X
Extrinsic reward systems		X	X
Training investments	X	X	X
Technological Factors			
Complexity for users	X		X
Compatibility with existing systems	X	X	X
Relative improvement over existing system (accuracy and timeliness)	X	X	X
Relevance to managers' decisions			X
Task Characteristics			
Uncertainty / lack of goal clarity	X	X	X
Variety			
Worker autonomy	X		
Worker responsibility	X	X	
External Environment			
Heterogeneity of demands	X		
Competition	X		
Environmental uncertainty	X		
External Communications	X		

Table 3.2. **Effect of Variables that Influenced ABC Implementation at GM**

Each cell contains the observed influence of the variable on the implementation stage [1] and a brief reference to the evidence that supports the claim. Factors in *italics* are those that emerged from the case analysis and were not identified initially as a candidate variable (Table 3.1).

CONTEXTUAL FACTOR	Initiation	Adoption	Adaptation	Acceptance
Individual Characteristics Disposition toward change/ *Intrinsic reward in change*	+: sponsor desire to make a difference		+: role of CPC leading change	
Job Tenure/ Process Knowledge		+: design skills and user buy-in		
Role Involvement	+: centrality to Comptroller's job	+: centrality to Director's job	-: ABC design owners slowed commonization	
Informal support (e.g., sponsors, champions)	+: Pontiac Comptroller	+: CPC Director of Finance -: limited opportunity for debate	+: CPC Director of Finance	+ ABC User's Group
Organizational Factors Centralization	-: Cooney Report	-: CSMC slow assessment +: pilot study built support	+: commonization	+: "blitz" as codification of simple implementation -: "blitz" as means of satisfying requirements
Functional specialization	+: role of GMR +/-: parallel experiments -: specialists can't approach problem with clean slate		-: innovations originated with multi disciplinary local teams	+: common cost systems committee
Internal communications/ *Horizontal versus Vertical*	+: horizontal discussion among stamping plants -: threatened traditional vertical communications	-: horizontal discussion threatened controlled experiments of pilot study	+: vertical communications aimed at supporting rather than directing local teams	+: CCL 2860
Training investments	+: theory focus, aim to persuade about problem	+: codified implementation	+: shift to ABM from ABC	+: implementation versus use and maintenance training

1. Four of Kwon and Zmud's (1987) six stages of implementation are considered.

Table 3.2. (continued): Effect of Variables that Influenced ABC Implementation at GM

CONTEXTUAL FACTOR	Initiation	Adoption	Adaptation	Acceptance
Technological Factors				
Complexity for users	+: pragmatic	+: compared to alternatives		
Compatibility with existing systems/ *Across ABC systems*	+: failure to address 'fit' of ABC with other systems			
Representational accuracy of model		+: intuitive appeal	+: standardization	
Relative improvement over existing system (accuracy and timeliness)	+: product cost changes	+: pilot study verification of product cost changes	+: negative effect of commonization	
Relevance to managers' decisions/ *Compatibility with firm strategies*		+: decision-support focus of pilot study		+: software modifications to support new ABM objectives
Task Characteristics				
Uncertainty / lack of goal clarity	+: challenge, using expertise	-: subjectivity in design		
Variety	-: Cooney Rept., excessive			+: lack of task variety in maintenance; "drudgery"
Worker autonomy	+: freedom to design model	-: subjectivity in design	+: plant originate innovations	
Worker responsibility/ *Personal Risk in task outcomes*	-: Cooney Report			
External Environment				
Heterogeneity of demands	+: ABC value linked to process/product diversity +: site of innovations		+: site of innovations	
Competition	+: threats of divestiture			
Environmental uncertainty	+: threats of divestiture	+: threats of divestiture -: turbulence within plant +: Smith's talk to NAA		
External Communications/Role of External Experts	+: SAC, Cooper and Kaplan		+: benchmarking other firms	-: auditor's preference for standardization before use

technology emerges --- namely, the greater reliance on external communications to validate the usefulness of the approach when it is first considered and to calibrate progress after implementation is underway. Krumweide (1998) used survey data from a large sample of ABC adopters to test the hypothesis that different factors influence the likelihood that a firm successfully negotiates the sequential stages of implementation and found general support for the premise.

This overview of "key success factors" along the dynamic path of implementation is meant to provide a high level framing for the remaining chapters, which focus on 21 individual ABC projects that were part of the later stages of routinization and infusion of ABC in these firms. Our examination of ABC development teams and the way the teams interacted with local managers to produce successful (or not) ABC models comprehends settings with different levels of team autonomy and technical skill, different beliefs about the importance of the task, different investments in team training, and different environmental circumstances (e.g., competitive setting). Moreover, our selection of projects reflects an attempt to investigate ABC system maturation. Thus we move from corporate headquarters where, for large firms, the decision to adopt ABC is typically taken, to field operations, where the hard work of developing and maintaining informative models takes place.

NOTES

[1] This section is taken from Anderson (1995), and portions are reprinted with permission from Anthony Atkinson, current editor of the *Journal of Management Accounting Research.*

[2] Stamping plants produce a wide variety of metal parts, including internal stampings (e.g. oil pan) as well as external automotive body panels (e.g. hood, fender), for automotive assembly plants. Transfer presses hold multiple dies and perform a series of stamping operations within one machine with automatic, internal transfer of the part from one die to the next.

[3] Although managers could conceivably manage operations better with improved cost data, they were restricted to using traditional product costs in all reports to central office that included product costs. Managers' willingness to expend resources on experiments that had limited official use is unusual.

[4] A pilot study conducted in summer, 1986, examined the relative indirect resource usage of two similar car hoods that had dramatically different production volumes but identical allocated unit overhead costs. The study's results motivated the plant manager to endorse a comprehensive study of product costs in one of the plant's two major facilities. The resulting ABC model, which was developed by a multi-disciplinary team using spreadsheets on a personal computer, was completed in late 1987. See Beaujon and Singhal (1990) and Cooper (1990a) for details.

[5] We use the term "ABC" to describe the Pontiac system; however, the language of "activities" did not emerge until later as a response to changing needs for cost information.

[6]Interestingly, as the word is used in memos from the period, "user" typically referred to the local ABC design teams. Later, the word was used in the more conventional style of the IT literature to refer to managers who would use ABC data as an input to decision-making. For example, local ABC Design Teams were exhorted to "identify user needs for product costs" to ensure that they designed ABC models that could meet these needs. However, even in 1993 the corporation sponsored "ABC User Group Meetings" that were attended primarily by plant-level ABC Designers and Group-level Liaisons.

[7]Minutes of the first CSMC workgroup meeting on January 11, 1989, confirm this view, stating, "the cost sub-team exists to focus on the application of ABC, determine benefits, select pilots, develop refinements, and draw conclusions about the program."

[8]This goal reflects an anticipation of managerial resistance to change rather than union or worker resistance. In keeping with traditional uses of cost data, there was never any expectation that ABC data would be used by shop floor workers. Even by 1993, the Vice President of Finance for NAO indicated that there was no involvement of the union in ABC implementation, and although shop floor workers had occasionally participated on local ABC system design teams, typically shop floor workers were unaware of ABC because they were not expected to use cost data in their jobs.

[9]Three reasons were cited for the failure of ABC to be used at the plant level. First, managers found the ABC model too complex for anything other than basic product costing and had difficulty relating it to operating decisions. Second, because the ABC model used as inputs actual costs from 1986, the data was viewed as "useless" by the time the model was completed in mid-1987. "There was a perception, because the traditional system reports costs as of that year or that point in time, that it was better than old ABC product costs." Finally, after Pontiac's Comptroller moved to CPC as the ABC Sponsor, the system was not maintained. The Director of NAO Product Costing commented that "Pontiac was actually the least successful in terms of providing data... the Pontiac location lost its momentum... [because] they believed that the plant would be closed."

[10]The ABC Designer recalled, "some were volunteers and some agreed after a lot of arm twisting."

[11]One plant bowed out of the study. It was implementing major changes to the manufacturing process and management believed that this turmoil precluded developing a meaningful ABC model.

[12] The most controversial ABC failure occurred at the sole auto assembly plant in the pilot sample. Plant management contended that the plant produced one product, could do little to affect its cost structure, was predominantly influenced by labor costs, and consequently was well served by a labor-based system. The cost workgroup disagreed, arguing that product and process variation was significant when on considered option packages. Unlike other ABC failures, that occurred in relatively small plants, the Council believed that ABC was limited as a corporate strategy if it could not be used in assembly plants, which represent a major portion of the vehicle production process. The team was asked to implement ABC in a second assembly plant. Subsequently, this implementation failed for similar reasons, and the issue of ABC for assembly plants was tabled indefinitely.

[13]The "blitz" approach was pioneered as a cost effective means of implementing a simple ABC system. The local design team was instructed to collect data that was likely to be used in an ABC design, given their production processes. Then the ABC Sponsor and CPC's Group Liaison traveled to the plant and spent a week teaching the team ABC concepts and helping

them design a rudimentary ABC model. Subsequently, the local team refined the model. Later the blitz method was applied to plants which met criteria related to plant size, process complexity, and data availability.

[14]Perhaps the most exciting news of the meeting, which raised a cheer from the crowd was the announcement by the Director of Current Product Cost NAO that with complete implementation of ABC, the company's auditors had approved the switch to ABC product costs for purposes of component inventory valuation in 1994. Up until then, the auditor's had resisted ABC as a method of inventory valuation because they wanted to switch methods at one time, not year by year as new implementations became available. For the first time, ABC would be fully integrated with financial accounting.

[15]There is not a one to one relationship between plants (single physical locations) and ABC models because some plants are subdivided for ABC modeling purposes.

[16] An interesting aside is that the firm that was using that same software as that used by GM was viewed favorably. The memo summarizing the evaluation of the four proposals noted that because GM was in the forefront of implementation, this firm was likely to be pushed for software enhancements that Chrysler would also value.

[17] An issue that was under debate in the task force was whether to use a strategy of quickly implementing "partial" ABC models, which would be enriched during subsequent annual maintenance tasks, or whether to develop "full" models from the outset. The head of PFA argued forcefully against partial models, saying that they would be viewed by operations managers as one-time, special cost studies rather than as a substantive change in cost management methods.

[18]See Kwon and Zmud (1987) for a review of empirical studies of IT implementation.

[19] See Bostrom and Heinen (1977); Ginzberg (1981); Markus (1983,1984); Mumford (1983); Ives and Olson (1984); Leonard-Barton and Kraus (1985) and Kanter, Stein and Jick (1992).

[20] See Ginzberg (1981); Markus (1983, 1984); Leonard-Barton and Kraus (1985); Zuboff (1988); Armstrong (1990a, 1990b); Morton (1991); Kanter, Stein and Jick (1992).

[21] See Robey (1981); Franz and Robey (1984); Markus and Robey (1988), and Fireworker and Zirkel (1990).

[22]Kwon and Zmud's (1987) sequential stages were modified by Cooper and Zmud (1990). We use Cooper and Zmud's stages, however the general framework is that of the earlier Kwon and Zmud study.

Chapter 4

INFLUENCES ON, AND CHARACTERISTICS OF, THE ABC DEVELOPMENT TEAMS

1. OVERVIEW

Katzenberg and Smith (1993) define a team as "a small number of people with complementary skills who are committed to a common purpose, performance goals, and approach for which they hold themselves mutually accountable." Teams are considered effective organizing units because of the flexibility they offer. Unlike large organizations, teams can be assembled quickly and can focus on performing specific tasks. Once tasks are completed, team members can return to their regular job responsibilities or be redeployed to another team. Teams can range from supervised workgroups that perform routine, repetitive tasks, to those that are self-managed and involved with high level decision responsibility. According to a survey done by Lawler, Mohrman and Ledford (1995) teams have proliferated to such an extent that 68% of the Fortune 1000 firms use self-managed teams as a work unit.

Implementing management innovations such as ABC usually involves project and development teams. Unlike workgroups, project and development teams are cross-functional involving designers, operators, cost analysts, engineers, and functional managers. These individuals coalesce to perform a non-routine task of limited scope and duration. By including a diverse set of perspectives, development teams have the potential to generate new ideas or derive novel solutions to complex problems.

While project teams have become one of the organizing units of choice, very little has been written about them. For instance, how does the team form and how are members chosen? What mix of skills and training is desirable? What is the nature of the task the teams perform? What kinds of outcomes are measured? Finally, what external and internal factors influence team performance?

In this and the subsequent chapter, we address these questions within our ABC implementation context based on interviews and surveys.[1] We begin by discussing representative recollections of how some individuals became team members. Next, we present a systematic profile of the teams based on the types of plants in which they operated. Then we discuss the team task and present data about the ABC models designed. The chapter concludes with a discussion of how managers might use this information in designing more effective ABC teams. In the next chapter, we discuss team performance measures and develop a model that links intragroup and other factors that influence the performance of the teams as they develop their first ABC model.

2. BECOMING A TEAM MEMBER

Our interviews revealed several ways in which employees became ABC team members. First, some were told by supervisors that their next assignment was to become a member of an ABC team. Almost all were chosen based on specific knowledge or experience. For instance, team members told us:

I was asked and said OK. I really didn't mind because I felt like I knew enough about ABC from reading text book type information that I might be able to help the plant. They seemed to want someone who had a cost background. And that's basically why I was willing to do it.

I was picked primarily because we needed someone who knew operations...I was an industrial engineer who had knowledge, of indirect labor activities.

I was originally on the floor. I just finished my degree in finance and I had an interview for an accounting job that basically fell through. The controller knew I was out there and he pulled me up here and asked me if I wanted to do it.

I was selected because I have a decent level of computer skills. I had some background in general ledgers so I could understand some of the finance aspects of it. And I was fairly well known in the plant among the people we'd be getting the information from.

Some supervisors charged with forming the team, simply asked for volunteers. One volunteer stated:

I asked for it...what sparked my interest was the newness of it. I like change. I like improvement. And I saw where this was a new area for me to come in and that it would help educate me, too.

Another aspect of selection was how the ABC team membership was "sold" to prospective members. In some cases, supervisors were enthusiastic and in others they were not:

> My supervisor was excited about it. He was really gung-ho about it...as a matter of fact he was my partner...and he was a plant superintendent. He and I did all of the models together, and the camaraderie was great.

> My boss came to me and said, 'You will be on the ABC team.'

The individuals we interviewed all had skills in cost analysis, finance, manufacturing, industrial engineering, or computing. Many had been employed by their organizations for some time and were selected because of their knowledge or connections with others in the plant. All had received some form of ABC training.

Within firms, we could not discern any systematic method by which individuals were selected nor any systematic differences between the firms. The Corporate ABC team allowed plants a great deal of latitude when selecting team members. While this approach is reasonable since local plants often have a better idea of who is interested and available, it is also plausible that there is an "optimal" mix of team members within each plant that have the necessary skills and experience. It remains an open question whether corporate oversight in staffing the teams might have on to different team compositions for each plant.

In the next section, we use data from *the Survey of Activity Based Costing Implementation* (Appendix II) to develop a more systematic and comprehensive profile of the characteristics of ABC development teams at our research sites.

3. CHARACTERISTICS OF ABC DEVELOPMENT TEAMS

Based on discussions with corporate ABC personnel and ABC plant level team leaders at our research sites, we organize the discussion of team composition based on two factors - whether plants used an *external consultant* to aid them in ABC model development, and the *degree of competition* plants faced (see Figure 4.1).

Figure 4.1. **Factors Influencing ABC Teams**

	Company A (External Consultants Absent)	Company B (External Consultants Present)
Core Manufacturing (Lower Competition)		
Non Core Manufacturing (Higher competition)		

3.1 The Presence or Absence of an External Consultant

Company A did not employ external consultants, while Company B used external consultants at every plant. At Company A, teams identified activity centers and selected cost drivers and were essentially developing ABC models from the ground up. The Corporate ABC group provided some guidance on choosing parameters based on shared information from common processing environments. One ABC team member at Company A characterized their approach in the following way:

Here at the plant, we really just started from scratch and said, make it as you go or handle it as it comes along.

Another ABC team leader stated,

The approach was to teach people concepts, demonstrate to them the advantages of ABC, give them some guidelines on approaches to it … then go out and do it and do your own inventing where necessary.

At Company B, external consultants supported ABC implementation at each plant. Using this approach, a consultant from a major accounting firm guided the use of a design template that was superimposed on each site. The template consisted of a standardized corporate activity dictionary[2] and restricted choices regarding activity centers and cost drivers. In rare cases, a plant was permitted to add a site-specific activity, but this required corporate approval. While there was some leeway in selecting first and second stage cost drivers the relation between activities and cost drivers was largely pre-determined. One ABC team member stated,

> They're going to do a lot of the ground work up at Corporate and then just send us a model so there's not so much grunt work here.

But not all team members agreed with this approach,

> The standardization is good for the fact of expediting, [and] getting models updated... but you know, I think some individuality is lost.

3.2 Degree of Competition

A second factor was the degree of competition faced by different types of manufacturing plants *within* each company. Recall that in both companies plants are considered *Core* and *Non-Core*. *Core* plants are captive to their respective corporations, face little outside competition, and historically, have been able to sell almost all products they could produce to the corporation. The relative level of competition that *Core* plants face is low. *Non Core* plants produce automobile components and face a great deal of competitive pressure that has resulted in outsourcing and plant closings. Compared to *Core* plants, the relative level of competition at *Non Core* plants is high.

As an indication of the differences in the level of competition, one *Core* plant manager said,

> We're an internal supplier. There's a certain amount of protection that you have...If I didn't have the logo in front of this building and I had to go sell my product at competitive prices to those car and truck assembly plants it would absolutely make a difference.

Comparatively, a manager within a *Non Core* plant stated the following,

> Being an electronics business the competition is outrageous, overseas and even in companies here. Motorola would like our business. Radios are very competitive. You know everybody makes radios now, so it's tough.

4. PROFILING THE ABC TEAMS

In the next section we present a profile of the teams based on six characteristics:

- *team size* – number of individuals on the team[3]
- *team heterogeneity* – the functional areas represented on each team
- *organizational tenure* – the range of experience and knowledge about the organization in years
- *current plant tenure* – the range of experience and knowledge at their current plant in years
- *Level of general computer skills* – self reported level of computing skills on rating scales
- *Amount of ABC Training* – total hours of informal and informal training in ABC.

We present the results by whether the plant used a consultant and then at *Core* and *Non Core* plants within each company. Tables 4.1 Panels A and B and Table 4.2 Panels A and B and Figure 4.2 provide the details by Company (Company A – Consultant Absent or Company B Consultant Present) and by Core Status (Core – Lower Competition or Non Core – Higher Competition).

Figure 4.2. **Profile of ABC Teams at Both Companies**

	Company A (External Consultant Absent)	Company B External Consultant Present)
Core Manufacturing (Lower Competition)	Average Team Size: 4.2* Organizational Tenure: 18.7 yrs Current Plant Tenure: 10.7 yrs Computer Skills: 3.21 yrs ABC team training: 27.4 hrs	Average Team Size: 4.8 Organizational Tenure: 13.3 yrs Current Plant Tenure: 7.4 yrs Computer Skills: 3.45 yrs ABC team training: 33.4 hrs
Non Core Manufacturing (Higher competition)	Average Team Size: 3.8 Organizational Tenure: 15.9 yrs Current Plant Tenure: 9.3 yrs Computer Skills: 3.70 ABC team training: 48.2 hrs	Average Team Size: 3.0 Organizational Tenure: 12.5 yrs Current Plant Tenure: 9.5 yrs Computer Skills: 3.92 ABC team training: 30.6 hrs

*All numbers are averages

4.1 Team Size and Heterogeneity

For Company A, the average number of team members surveyed in the *Core* versus *Non Core* plants was 4.2 and 3.8, respectively.[4] Six types of employees are represented between *Core* and *Non Core* plants with the majority of team members coming from Finance. Only one plant had Union representation on its team. Surprisingly, only one Manufacturing employee is represented across all *Core* and *Non Core* plants. This is unusual since knowledge of manufacturing seems critical for ABC development teams in this industry, and since consultants have tended to prescribe cross-functional teams.

For Company B, we observe a similar number of team members surveyed between *Core* (4.8) and *Non Core* (3.0) with a slightly larger average number of team members in the *Core* plants than in Company A, and a slightly smaller number in the *Non Core* plants. The largest teams were in engine and transmission plants, both highly complex task environments for both firms. No Human Resource personnel were represented on Company B and similar to Company A, only one plant used a Union employee. Interestingly, five manufacturing employees were represented on five teams, three at *Core* plants and two at *Non Core* plants at Company B.

Also we note that between both companies the number of different types of employees is lower in *Non Core* teams than *Core* teams with Company A having five functional areas represented in their *Core* teams and only four represented in *Non Core* teams. Similarly for Company B, only three types of employees are represented in *Non Core* teams but five types are distributed on *Core* teams. Teams were slightly larger in *Core* plants and in *Non Core* plants, but the difference was not significant.[5]

With these data in mind, what were the impressions of the size of the teams? One of the most consistent concerns expressed was that teams needed more members and that team sizes were not sufficient to get the job done in a timely manner. One of the team leaders expressed this passionately:

> My people work very hard. They work long hours. They work just about every Saturday. I've got them working maybe 1 out of 8 Sundays. They're here...I've got __ in at 5 a.m. I've got __ in at 7 a.m. They work until 6 p.m. So I know they are working hard. I also know they're bright...we don't have the manpower in this shop to do everything we need to do and because of that, I'm constrained to 'cheap charlie' the ABC effort. I would love to have two guys, full-time doing business studies, doing opportunity cost analyses, and doing all sorts of analyses with ABC.

4.2 Organizational Tenure

Another characteristic was how long ABC team members had been with their companies in general (organizational tenure) and their current plant (plant tenure) in particular.

Table 4.1. **Factors Comprising Group Composition Variable for Company A, ABC Development Teams: Descriptive Statistics [Means and Standard Deviations ( )] (Panel A, Company A)**

Company A: Plant Number	Team Size	Team Heterogeneity: Functional Expertise/Job Experience					
	Number of Team Members	Finance	Industrial Engineering	Manu-facturing	Human Resources	Systems	Union Employee
Core Plants:							
Plant A1 (Engine)	5	1	2		1	1	
Plant A2 (Engine)	2	2					
Plant A3 (Transmission)	7	7					
Plant A4 (Foundry)	4	3				1	
Plant A5 (Stamping)	3	2		1			
Total Surveyed	21						
Core Average:	4.2 (1.92)	3.0	0.4	0.2	0.2	0.4	
Non Core Plants:							
Plant A6 (Components)	6*	2				2	1
Plant A7 (Components)	3	3					
Plant A8 (Components)	4	4					
Plant A9 (Components)	2	1		1			
Total Surveyed	15						
Non Core Average:	3.8 (1.71)	2.5		0.2		0.5	0.2
Total Both Cores	36						
All Plants Average	4.0 (1.73)	2.8	0.2	0.1	0.1	0.4	0.1

* One subject failed to indicate department.

Table 4.1. **Factors Comprising Team Composition Variable of Company B, ABC Development Teams: Descriptive Statistics [Means and Standard Deviations ( )] (Panel B, Company B)**

Company B: Plant Number	Team Size	Team Heterogeneity: Functional Expertise/Job Experience					
	Number of Team Members	Finance	Industrial Engineering	Manu-facturing	Human Resources	Systems	Union Employee
Core Plants:							
Plant B1 (Engine)	9*	5	1	1		1	
Plant B2 (Engine)	5	2	1			2	
Plant B3 (Transmission)	6†	4				1	1
Plant B4 (Foundry)	2			1			
Plant B5 (Stamping)	2	2					
Total Surveyed	24						
Core Average:	4.8 (2.95)	2.6	0.4	0.6		0.8	0.2
Non Core Plants:							
Plant B6 (Components)	2	1					
Plant B7 (Components)	4	3	1	1			
Plant B8 (Components)	2	2					
Plant B9 (Components)	3	2					
Non Core Average:	3.0 (1.15)	2.2	0.2	0.2			
Total Surveyed	11						
Total, Both Cores	35						
All Plants Average:	3.9 (2.42)	2.4	0.3	0.4	0	0.4	0.1

* One subject failed to indicate department.

† The union employee did not complete an ABC Developer Survey.

Table 4.2. Organizational and Current Job Tenure of ABC Development Teams: Descriptive Statistics [Means and Standard Deviations ( )] (Panel A, Company A)

Company A Plant Number	Organizational Tenure: Years of Company Experience	Current Job Tenure: Years of Experience at Plant	General Computer Skills	Total ABC Class Hours
Core Plants:				
Plant A1 (Engine)	20.8 (8.3)	9.8 (7.9)	3.67	48.0
Plant A2 (Engine)	23.0 (9.9)	17.0 (18.4)	2.50	40.0
Plant A3 (Transmission)	16.1 (7.9)	11.7 (9.4)	2.86	7.4
Plant A4 (Foundry)	16.0 (10.6)	5.2 (3.6)	3.89	24.0
Plant A5 (Stamping)	22.0 (8.7)	13.0 (1.0)	3.11	24.0
Core Average:	18.7 (8.4)	10.7 (8.3)	3.21	28.7
Non Core Plants:				
Plant A6 (Components)	11.2 (9.6)	8.2 (6.6)	3.61	48.0
Plant A7 (Components)	13.3 (9.1)	5.0 (0.0)	3.78	44.0
Plant A8 (Components)	22.0 (8.3)	16.0 (15.1)	4.08	45.0
Plant A9 (Components)	21.5 (5.0)	5.0 (1.4)	3.33	56.0
Non Core Average:	15.9 (9.3)	9.3 (9.3)	3.70	48.2
All Plants Average:	17.5 (8.8)	10.1 (8.6)	3.43	37.3

Table 4.2. Organizational and Current Job Tenure of ABC Development Teams: Descriptive Statistics [Means and Standard Deviations ( )] (Panel B, Company B)

Company B Plant Number	Organizational Tenure: Years of Experience at Company	Current Job Tenure: Years of Experience at Plant	General Computer Skills	Total ABC Class Hours
Core Plants:				
Plant B1 (Engine)	11.8 (11.4)	5.4 (9.3)	3.56	22
Plant B2 (Engine)	9.6 (8.6)	6.8 (9.4)	3.73	83
Plant B3 (Transmission)	13.8 (10.9)	12.4 (12.4)	4.13	25
Plant B4 (Foundry)	28.0 (*)	7.0 (*)	3.33	12
Plant B5 (Stamping)	20.0 (11.3)	2.0 (1.4)	2.50	20
Core Average:	13.3 (10.8)	7.4 (9.6)	3.45	32.4
Non Core Plants:				
Plant B6 (Components)	12.5 (0.7)	12.5 (0.7)	3.83	14
Plant B7 (Components)	12.0 (5.4)	4.2 (4.6)	4.67	68
Plant B8 (Components)	17.5 (14.8)	17.5 (14.8)	4.00	3
Plant B9 (Components)	10.0 (3.0)	9.3 (4.0)	3.17	38
Non Core Average:	12.5 (6.3)	9.5 (7.6)	3.92	30.6
All Plants Average:	13.0 (9.4)	8.2 (8.9)	3.66	31.7

Organizational tenure for Company A's team members averaged 18.7 years in *Core* plants and 15.9 in *Non Core* plants. While at Company B, team members spent 13.3 years at *Core* plants and 12.5 in *Non Core* plants. Overall, Company A's team members had more years of experience in their organization than those at Company B. An analysis of variance revealed that organizational tenure differed significantly between Company A and Company B with Company A team members have longer tenure than those at Company B.

4.3 Current Plant Tenure

The average years of experience for team members at their current plant for Company A was 10.7 years for *Core* plant teams and 9.3 for *Non Core* plant teams. Company B reports fewer years of experience at the plant with the *Core* team average being 7.4 years and *Non Core* average of 9.5 years. Overall, current plant tenure is slightly less on average for Company B than Company A. Analysis of variance showed no differences by implementation approach or degree of competition.

4.4 General Computing Skills

General computing skills were assessed using answers to three questions. Each was rated on a 1-5 scale, with a "1" indicating "strongly disagree" and a "5"indicating "strongly agree." The questions used were: (a) "I am a skilled user of at least one piece of spreadsheet software for personal computers (e.g., Lotus 1-2-3, Quattro Pro or Microsoft Excel)," (b) "I am a skilled user of at least one piece of database software for personal computers (e.g., Paradox, FoxPro, D-Base, or Microsoft Access)", and (c) "I am a skilled user of at least one piece of word processing for personal computers (e.g., WordPerfect, Word, Volkswriter)."

The average self-reported scores showed that overall, team members at both companies rated their skills between a "3" and a "4" essentially agreeing that they had a reasonable level of computing skills. See Table 4.2. Analysis of variance showed that *Non Core* plants (those facing greater competition) reported significantly greater general computer skills than those at *Core* plants. There were no differences between companies.

4.5 ABC Team Training

Three types of training were assessed: (a) Degree-granting educational programs, (b) Non-degree courses offered by external providers, and (c) Non-degree courses offered by the company. Team members were asked to determine the total number of class hours associated with each type of training. The level of training was assessed using the total hours of ABC training across the three types. While almost all team members across both companies went to headquarters for training there was a wide variety in the types and intensity of training as discussed below,

My boss gave me a book to read. I think it was the *Common Cents?* book. And so I started reading it and then I read a couple of articles in some magazines.

I had 30 to 36 hours of training from seminars and classrooms within the corporation. As I said, my involvement from teaching standard cost has led me through a lot of literature on my own.

We went to Detroit for training for a week. Cooper and Kaplan and one of our controllers lead the training.

Our team went to Highland Park for two days to basically give us an overview of what ABC was. A consulting firm did the overview.

Our analysis found that teams in *Non Core* plants had a significantly higher level of training than those in *Core* plants.

4.6 Summary of Team Characteristics

4.6.1 Company A Versus Company B

The size of ABC teams is comparable between companies. Both Companies ABC development teams were dominated by finance personnel, although Company B's teams were composed of more manufacturing personnel. Employees in Company A's teams tend to have a slightly longer history in their organization and their current plants than do Company B's.

4.6.2 Core Versus Non Core Teams

Core teams between companies have larger teams than *Non Core* teams, and *Non Core* teams have less functional area diversity than *Core* teams. The level of organizational experience is higher for *Core* teams compared to *Non Core* teams, but there is no clear pattern for current plant experience. General computing skills are significantly higher for *Non Core* teams compared to *Core* teams, as is the total number of ABC hours of training.

Both of these factors indicate that both companies chose long-time employees to be ABC developers. Such employees are good choices for team members since they have the advantage of having more knowledge, knowing more people and understanding the way the organization works.

4.6.3 The Task of the ABC Teams

The principal task of the teams was to design ABC models that linked the resources, activities and cost drivers of an organization. Organizations that have complex production and support processes, and manufacture numerous product lines usually require more work on the part of the team to model. ABC development teams break this complexity down as follows: activities, 1st stage cost drivers, activity centers, and 2nd stage cost drivers and ultimately derive component and product costs.

5. MANAGERIAL IMPLICATIONS FOR TEAM DESIGN

As organizations make greater use of team structures they are faced with the dilemma of how to manage their human resources. While teams can be a very effective means by which tasks can be accomplished, the more teams that are formed the greater the difficulty of finding and allocating talent to these teams. The impression we received when studying both companies was that plant controllers who were usually involved in selecting team members did not have the luxury of systematically deciding their optimal team for the ABC task. This is not to say that those who were chosen were not highly skilled and competent people, but rather that for many teams, a different mix of skills and even more personnel might have been more effective.

It is impossible for us to say whether a different mix of people would have produced different results; however, in some cases teams were disproportionately comprise of finance rather than manufacturing personnel. Since the ABC initiative was launched through Finance, the use of Finance personnel isn't surprising; however, manufacturing personnel are more intimately involved with the everyday workings of the shop floor and may have made different cost assignment choices as a result. Our recommendation for the future would be to seek a greater balance between manufacturing and finance people.

In addition to a better mix of manufacturing and finance people on teams, it also seems necessary to incorporate employees from other functional areas perhaps with another steering committee be formed at each plant. Such a steering committee wouldn't be directly involved with developing the ABC models, but rather could serve as an advisory and marketing group for the efforts of the ABC team. While there were efforts at each plant to "sell" ABC, much of this activity was done at the beginning of the initiative and not during or at the end of the process.

Apart from the kinds of functional expertise, team size seemed to be an issue in almost all of the plants we visited. Our data show that the average team size was around four employees across both companies, and in some instances teams consisted of only two members. In particular for companies building ABC models from scratch these team sizes seem inadequate to complete the task in a timely fashion. Timely completion of ABC models is an extremely important performance variable because if the task takes too long, other organizational members either forget that the innovation is occurring or begin to lose confidence in the process.

To resolve the team size issue, we suggest that organizations budget more human resources rather they think they need so that the initiative will not lose momentum. Perhaps an algorithm for team size could be developed based on an initial assessment by a Corporate group of the size and complexity of the task for each specific plant. Initial measures of size could include the number of products produced, the square footage of the plant or the plant's headcount. Suggesting greater resource allocation for teams should not be construed as naiveté on our part – we realize that human resources are severely constrained in these times. But, if management innovations such as ABC are important enough to implement, then both team members and the rest of the organization should have confidence in the process and the development of timely outcomes.

A strength of most of the ABC project teams was the work experience of team members at both their respective companies and their respective plants. On average, ABC team members had close to 18 years of organizational experience and over 10 years of current plant experience. Such experience should have translated into knowing one's way around the plant, efficiency in the task of building the ABC model, and understanding the underlying political structure and context.

The level of computer skills seemed quite adequate and the only difficulty that teams encountered was in the software (Profit Manager™) that was developed to aid them in running their models. While Profit Manager was a real innovation for its time, it was very slow and was difficult to use when data were imported from other systems (e.g. accounting ledgers). Over time, many advances have been made in software technology and these issues have diminished. Finally, the amount and kind of ABC training varied significantly by person. In some cases, team members had extensive training including MBA degrees with ABC coursework while others had on-sight training.. Certainly much more standardization of ABC training is warranted.

In the next chapter, we extend our discussion on the team process by looking at the effects of intra-team dynamics and how these and other factors influenced the development of the ABC models and their timely completion.

NOTES

[1] The chapter presents results related to 18 of the 21 plants that we visited. Three sites are excluded since they included significant non-manufacturing activities and thus are not easily comparable to the other sites.

[2] An activity dictionary defines admissible "activities" that are cost objects in the 1st of a two-stage cost assignment.

[3] Data in the tables represent ABC team members from whom we were able to collect data. In total, data from 70 ABC developers (36 for Company A and 34 for Company B) are reported. The data represent all current ABC developers in some plants while at others we do not have the entire team. Individuals who are not included were not available at the time of our plant visits. On average, we believe we have data from about 85% of all past and present ABC developers.

[4] Team sizes do not include the accounting firm consultants but do include those in each firm from their information technology divisions.

[5] 2 x 2 Analysis of Variance (ANOVAs) were run for each characteristic. The 5% level of significance was used to determine significant differences for main effects of company and *Core*.

Chapter 5

FACTORS INFLUENCING THE PERFORMANCE OF ABC TEAMS

1. OVERVIEW

In the previous chapter we discussed the process by which ABC teams were formed and described team characteristics. In this chapter, we probe more deeply into a key element of the team process and consider team functioning and team composition against a backdrop of extensive research on the effective use of teams in organizations.[1]

As mentioned previously, teams are being used for a multitude of tasks in organizations. However, the research literature tells us that some tasks are more or less amenable to team production and some tasks benefit more or less from diverse perspectives. Experts have argued that ABC implementation requires the diverse viewpoints of a multi-disciplinary team. A multi-disciplinary team is hypothesized to be better equipped to build an ABC model that reflects the use of resources in different parts of the organization and more likely to elicit cooperation from other employees who are asked to share information about their work. In spite of these claims, there is evidence in the research literature that teams can be a costly means of organizing work. Teams may take longer to reach decisions (although the decisions may be of higher quality), and teamwork imposes coordination costs associated with managing the actions of team members.

It is important to understand whether ABC implementation is an environment that favors team processes when the costs and benefits of team production are considered together. It is also important, for ABC projects that are less successful, to disentangle failures in team processes from technical design failures or inappropriate use of ABC. In this chapter we focus on team effects on ABC implementation outcomes. Understanding effects of team dynamics and team composition may lead to greater efficiency and effectiveness in developing and implementing ABC models. At the end of the chapter, we suggest how ABC team leaders, controllers and managers might use these findings to improve the performance of management innovation teams.

2. THE MODEL AND RESEARCH EXPECTATIONS

There is very little systematic research on factors that influence the performance of teams charged with implementing management innovations. Our goal in developing the ABC teams model is to explain the ABC teams' performance. Specifically, we address two general research questions.

What factors:

1. influence the complexity of ABC models; and,
2. the time it takes to develop an initial ABC model.

The starting point for any model is the selection of independent factors or variables that ultimately influence the outcome or dependent variables. We chose the independent and dependent variables based on over 50 years of research on small group behavior, previous studies on ABC implementation and pre-study interviews with our host companies.[2] The independent variables are grouped into three categories:

- *Team inputs* such as team size, heterogeneity, ABC training, and use of an external consultant. Team size and heterogeneity are primarily the result of local managerial discretion. ABC training was typically sponsored by local management but some employees may have some training as a result of continuing education. The presence or absence of a consultant was a decision made at the corporate ABC level.

- *External factors*, such as the level of competition faced by the firm. While the intensity of competition varies from plant to plant, *Core* facilities seem to face less outside competition than *Non Core* facilities.

- *Measures of team dynamics*, such as the perception of conflict resolution, task significance and team cohesion. These variables are behavioral constructs whose effects vary depending on team inputs, competition and their own interrelationships.

The two dependent variables, *model complexity* and *time to develop the initial ABC model* were chosen for the following reasons. First many managers have expressed surprise and concern over the level of effort required to develop and implement a functioning ABC model.

In some cases ABC implementation failure has been attributed to this unexpected level of effort (see Ness and Cucuzza, 1995). Second, many ABC models flounder because they are too complex. As model complexity increases, constructing the model becomes more difficult. Perhaps most importantly, more complex models are harder to comprehend and use (Anderson, 1995).

In the following sections, we discuss how the variables are interrelated. These relations are stated as specific *research expectations* that are statistically tested. In the model, each research expectation is shown as a path linking one variable to the next. The model specifying the full set of relations among all of the independent and dependent variables is depicted in Figure 5.1.

2.1 The Effects of Team Size, Team Heterogeneity and the Presence of An External Consultant on Conflict Resolution

The first set of research expectations that we develop relate to factors that influence conflict resolution. Hackman (1987) has noted that the ability to resolve conflicts is often a characteristic of well-functioning teams.[3] Organizations must decide how large and diverse to make their teams. Teams that are too small may not have enough mental and physical resources to accomplish their tasks. Teams that are too large may be unmanageable. Regarding the ability to resolve conflicts, as team size increases, the potential for greater diversity of opinions, even for people of similar backgrounds also increases. Larger teams may exhibit greater team heterogeneity.[4] While diversity of opinion may challenge team members to consider other ideas, greater conflicts may arise over how to proceed with the task, and the scope of data to collect. In general, we expect that increases in both team size and heterogeneity make conflict resolution more difficult.[5]

Research Expectation 1: As team size increases, the team's ability to resolve conflicts decreases.

Research Expectation 2: As team heterogeneity increases, the team's ability to resolve conflicts decreases.

What about the role of the consultant in resolving conflicts? The presence of a consultant may or may not increase a team's ability to resolve conflicts.

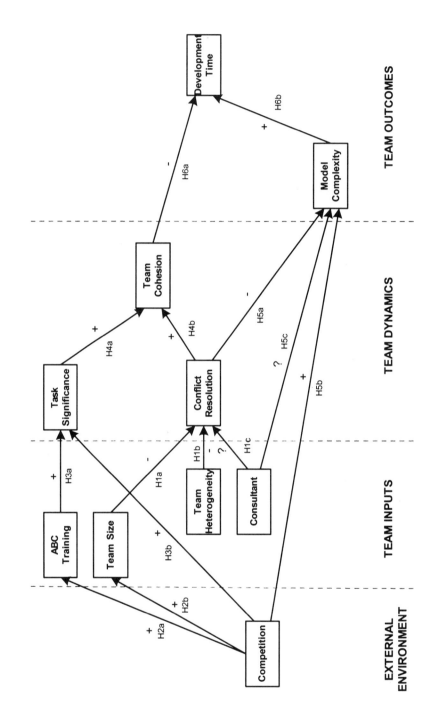

Figure 5.1. ABC Development Team's Model

However, in this context, the consultants at Company B used standardized templates that provided guidelines for developing ABC models. The use of templates may lead to fewer conflicts among team members about model parameters. In the "procedural form" of process consultation to resolve conflicts, standardized procedures and rules are used to overcome conflicts (Prein, 1984). At Company A, a decision was made not to use external consultants. This discussion leads to our third expectation.

Research Expectation 3: The presence of an external consultant using consulting procedures increases the team's ability to resolve conflicts.

2.2 The Effects of Competition on ABC Training and Team Size

The automobile industry is highly competitive. Research Expectations 4 and 5 are focused on how competition influences the amount of ABC training and team size. As discussed in the previous chapter, plants in our companies are exposed typically to different levels of competitive pressure. *Core* plants are those in which the corporation has invested heavily in capital equipment. Core plants are captive to their respective corporations, face little outside competition, and historically have been able to sell almost all products they could produce to the corporation. The relative level of competition that Core plants face is low. *Non Core* plants face a great deal of competitive pressure. Compared to Core plants, the relative level of competition at Non Core plants is high. Managers in Non Core plants are motivated to develop the most accurate cost models in order to be cost competitive. In the development of the ABC model, managers have discretion over the amount of technical ABC training and the number of personnel available for ABC teams.

At the local level, it is in each plant manager's best interest to invest greater resources in team input variables such as the amount of ABC training and team size based on perceived need. We expect these resources to vary based on the level of competition as reflected in the following research expectations:

Research Expectation 4: ABC Teams that face a high level of competition will have a greater level of ABC training than those that face a low level of competition.

Research Expectation 5: ABC Teams that face a high level of competition will have larger team sizes than those that face a low level of competition.

2.3 The Effects of ABC Training and Competition on Task Significance

Viewing any task as significant generally leads to higher levels of motivation (Hackman and Oldham, 1976; 1980).[6] Nothing is more debilitating than working on a task or project that individuals or teams view as unimportant or insignificant. In many cases, training to understand the nature and significance of the task is critical. Within our plants, training to educate team members was conducted locally and off-site by the corporate ABC group, the consultant or in classes.[7] ABC training was designed to help employees understand the technical aspects of ABC and its implications for more accurate product costing and resource allocation compared to traditional costing methods.[8] In addition, as teams face greater competition, greater cost pressure is felt and the salience of the ABC model-building task increases. The discussion suggests the following research expectations:

Research Expectation 6: As the level of ABC training increases, the perceived level of task significance increases.

Research Expectation 7: ABC Teams that face a high level of competition will experience a higher level of task significance than those that face a low level of competition.

2.4 The Effects of Task Significance and Conflict Resolution on Team Cohesion

One of the most influential group dynamics variables is group or team cohesion. Cohesive teams are often more satisfied and productive. Cohesion is defined as the commitment of members to the team task or the set of activities that the team must perform to achieve the group's goal (see Goodman, Ravlin and Schminke, 1987). Cohesiveness can be influenced by several factors. Two of the most important, however, are the degree to which team members are working toward a common goal and how well team members interact (see Goodman et al., 1987). Expectations 8 and 9 summarize the discussion.

Research Expectation 8: As the level of task significance increases, the level of ABC team cohesion increases.

Research Expectation 9: As the team's ability to resolve conflicts increases, so does the level of ABC team cohesion.

2.5 The Effects of Conflict Resolution, Competition, and External Consultants on Model Complexity

Kaplan and Cooper (1998) state that a goal of ABC model building is to develop a model that reflects operations in a parsimonious manner. In theory, designers should invest in model complexity up to the point where the marginal returns in improved information are equal to the cost of model development. In practice, it is difficult to know when this point is reached (Datar and Gupta, 1994 for more discussion). While we do not attempt to resolve this issue here, we do suggest that three factors play a role in determining ABC model complexity. These are the ability of the team to resolve team conflicts, the presence of an external consultant using process consulting procedures, and the perceived level of competition.[9]

Anderson (1995) documents the progression of one company from extremely complex models to more parsimonious models in the early prototyping of the ABC concept. The sites of this study, which implemented ABC after the prototyping stage, were familiar with the costs of model complexity. Indeed, a key feature of ABC training was to sensitize ABC team members to the importance of designing simple, yet useful models. Thus, if complex models emerge, we believe that it is either a response to a need for more discrimination among product costs (e.g., an outcome of competitive needs), or a failure of the team to reach compromises on what constitutes adequate, simple models. Ineffective conflict resolution surrounding issues such as how to reduce model complexity (e.g., number of activity centers, number of cost drivers) can result in compromises that leave model complexity excessively high.

Research Expectation 10: As the team's ability to resolve conflicts increases, ABC model complexity decreases.

As mentioned previously, the competition faced by Non Core plants is greater than that faced by Core plants. For Non Core plants, competing successfully means that they can offer products and services at prices below that of competitors. The decision to implement activity based costing was made at corporate headquarters with the objectives of improving the accuracy of product costs and providing plant managers data on the cost of operations and opportunities for improvement. The literature in activity based costing suggests that in many cases more accurate product costs are obtained as overhead support activities are broken down into finer components and are assigned to products using cost drivers that are correlated with resource usage (Cooper and Kaplan, 1998). Thus greater accuracy will occur as more activity centers and more first and second stage cost drivers are used to assign costs to products. We hypothesize that:

> **Research Expectation 11:** As the perceived level of external competition increases, ABC model complexity increases.

As mentioned previously, at Company A, ABC team members were permitted to choose the number and boundaries of activity centers, and first and second stage cost drivers. Some guidance on choosing parameters was provided by the Corporate ABC group that facilitated information sharing by ABC teams from common process environments. At Company B, consultants used implementation templates that were superimposed on plants of similar type. The template consisted of a standardized corporate activity dictionary.[10] In some cases a plant was permitted to add site-specific activities, however, design parameters were largely pre-determined. Through interviews, Company B stated that one of its goals was to be the low cost producer of products. The strategy of being the low cost producer increased the demand for more accurate costing information and thus, to reduce costs, consultants in Company B had to obtain more detailed information about its cost structure.[11] As more accurate costing information is required, ABC teams will create more complex models. This argument is reflected in the next expectation.

> **Research Expectation 12:** The presence of a low cost firm strategy increases ABC model complexity.

2.6 The Effects of Team Cohesion and ABC Model Complexity on the Time to Develop the Initial ABC Model

Research suggests a number of team effectiveness measures (see Hackman, 1987; DeLone and McLean, 1992 and Wageman,1995). Of the large number of effectiveness measures available, the most relevant for this study is Hackman's (1987) "speed to a solution of a problem." In this study, we operationalize this concept as the amount of *time (in months) to develop the initial ABC model*. This variable is significant because developing an effective ABC model was the key goal of the ABC team and a source of competitive advantage.

Previous research has found that the level of team cohesion (the commitment of members to the team task) is an important predictor of a team achieving its goals (see Gladstein, 1984; Goodman *et al.*, 1987). Building an

ABC model in these plants is a complex task and requires more effort and time. Since constructing a representative ABC model in as short a time as possible was the team goal, the following expectations are suggested:

Research Expectation 13: As the level of team cohesion increases, the time it takes to develop the initial ABC model decreases.

Research Expectation 14: As ABC model complexity increases, the time to develop the initial ABC model increases.

3. VARIABLE MEASUREMENT

3.1 Independent Variables

3.1.1 External Environment

The degree of competition was determined using a categorical variable based on whether a plant was a CORE (1) or a NON CORE (0) plant. As mentioned previously, core plants faced a lower level than non-core plants.

3.1.2 Team Inputs

We measure four aspects of team inputs: team size, team heterogeneity, the amount of ABC training and the presence or absence of a consultant.

3.1.3 Team Size

We measured team size by the number of plant employees assigned to the project (see Table 5.1, Panels A and B).[12] On average, for Company A (see Panel A, Table 5.1, Column 2), the number of team members was 4.0 ($\underline{s}$ = 1.73). Company B's teams (see Panel B, Table 5.1, Column 2) average 3.9 team members ($\underline{s}$ = 2.42). The largest teams were in the highly complex task environments of engine and transmission plants.

3.1.4 Team Heterogeneity

Team heterogeneity is a measure of the number of different functional departments represented by team members. As shown in Table 5.1 (Panel A, Column 5) at most four different types of functional areas are represented on teams at Company A. In four cases, Finance is the only functional area represented on a team.

At Company B (Table 5.1, Panel B, Column 3) a similar pattern is observed with a maximum of four different functional areas represented on a team. Of the 9 teams only two are composed of employees solely from Finance. At both companies, on average, two functional areas are represented.

3.1.5 Amount of ABC Training

The amount of training was obtained by summing the number of ABC class hours provided by the company or plant and through formal education for each of the team members divided by the number of team members in each plant. Accordingly, the construct measures the average level of training provided to each team member in a plant. Table 5.1 (Panel A, Column 6) shows that each ABC team member in Company A averaged 36.7 ($\underline{s}$ = 16.39) hours of training, while each member in Company B averaged 32.1 ($\underline{s}$ = 26.77) (Table 5.1, Panel B, Column 6).

3.1.6 Presence of a Consultant

Because plants in only one company used a consultant to help in their implementations, and the others did not, we used a categorical variable to indicate the presence of a consultant (1) or the absence of a consultant (0) in our analyses.[13]

3.1.7 Team Dynamics

Items comprising the three behavioral constructs related to team dynamics, task significance, conflict resolution and team cohesion are shown in Table 5.2. All questions were scored on a 5-point Likert scale anchored by "1", *strongly disagree*, and "5", *strongly agree*. Descriptive statistics are detailed for each construct in Table 5.3.[14]

Since reliability coefficients were satisfactory (as noted in the following sections), we obtained summated scales for each subject. These scores were then averaged across team members to obtain a measure for each plant. To assess the appropriateness of aggregation, we computed interrater reliability coefficients for each construct and plant (James, Demaree and Wolf 1984). Values above 0.60 indicate good agreement among judgments made by a group of judges on a variable in regard to a single target. Of the 54 coefficients computed, only 7 were below 0.60. Three of these were at a single plant (B5) where the team members appeared to disagree on all three constructs. Because of our small sample size, we decided to retain this plant, noting the disagreement among team members. Our results are not sensitive to our decision to retain plant B5 in our sample. See Table 5.4.

Table 5.1. **ABC Development Team Characteristics, Descriptive Statistics (Panel A, Company A)**

Plant Number	Number of Team Members*	Number of Full-Time Equivalent Team Members	Number of Team Members from Finance Dept.	Functional Departments Represented	Average ABC Class Hours per Team Member
Plant A1 (Engine)	5	1.55	1	4	48.0
Plant A2 (Engine)	2	0.20	2	1	40.0
Plant A3 (Transmission)	7	2.60	7	1	7.4
Plant A4 (Foundry)	4	1.30	3	2	17.5
Plant A5 (Stamping)	3	1.50	2	2	24.0
Plant A6 (Components)	6	5.00	2	3	48.0
Plant A7 (Components)	3	2.75	3	1	44.0
Plant A8 (Components)	4	2.20	4	1	45.0
Plant A9 (Components)	2	2.00	1	2	56.0
All Plants Median:	**4.0**	**2.0**	**2.0**	**2.0**	**44.0**
All Plants Average:	**4.0 (1.73)**	**2.1 (1.32)**	**2.8 (1.86)**	**1.9 (1.05)**	**36.7 (16.39)**

*Excludes consultants; ** One subject in Plant A6 failed to indicate department
( ) standard deviations

Table 5.1. **ABC Development Team Characteristics, Descriptive Statistics (Panel B: Company B)**

Plant Number	Number of Team Members*	Number of Full-Time Equivalent Team Members	Number of Team Members from Finance Dept.	Functional Departments Represented	Average ABC Class Hours per Team Member
Plant B1 (Engine)	9	5.70	5	4	22.0
Plant B2 (Engine)	5	3.75	2	3	83.2
Plant B3 (Transmission)	6	5.50	4	3	29.6
Plant B4 (Foundry)	2	1.75	0	2	12.0
Plant B5 (Stamping)	2	0.35	2	1	20.0
Plant B6 (Components)	2	1.75	1	2	14.0
Plant B7 (Components)	4	2.35	3	2	67.5
Plant B8 (Components)	2	1.25	2	1	3.0
Plant B9 (Components)	3	2.00	2	2	38.0
All Plants Median:	**3.0**	**2.0**	**2.0**	**2.0**	**22.0**
All Plants Average:	**3.9 (2.42)**	**2.7 (1.87)**	**2.3 (1.50)**	**2.2 (0.97)**	**32.1 (26.77)**

*Excludes consultants; ** One subject in Plant B3 failed to indicate department
( ) standard deviations

Table 5.2. Summary Statistics for Survey Items and Constructs

Construct	Survey items Anchors: 1 = strongly disagree; 5 = strongly agree	Item N	Item Mean	Standard Deviation	Cronbach's α
Task Significance			**3.4**	**0.81**	**0.89**
1.	A lot of people will be affected by how I do my job on ABC.	85	3.5	1.00	
2.	The future of this plant will be affected by how well I do my job on ABC.	79	3.0	1.09	
3.	Working on ABC gave me the opportunity to contribute something worthwhile to this plant.	84	3.7	0.91	
4.	The work I did on ABC was extremely meaningful to me.	86	3.7	0.94	
5.	My work on ABC had a visible effect on this plant.	86	3.1	1.12	
6.	As I performed my tasks on ABC, I could see the contribution I was making.	84	3.7	0.95	
Conflict Resolution			**4.0**	**0.59**	**0.76**
1.	On the ABC team, everyone's opinions were heard.	82	4.1	0.76	
2.	When a decision was required, every member of the ABC team was involved.	80	3.6	0.84	
3.	If a disagreement arose between ABC team members, the issue was dealt with in an open fashion.	80	4.0	0.71	
4.	When a disagreement arose between ABC team members everyone tried to find a workable solution.	79	4.0	0.68	
Team Cohesion			**3.9**	**0.81**	**0.80**
1.	When I was on the ABC team I felt that I was really a part of the group.	79	3.9	0.93	
2.	I looked forward to working with ABC team members each day.	82	3.8	0.89	
3.	There was a strong feeling of camaraderie among ABC team members.	83	3.9	0.90	

Note. Descriptive data for constructs averaged across all plants are shown in bold. Item statistics for all respondents are shown in regular font below the construct name.

Table 5.3. **Components of Team Process for ABC Development Teams, Descriptive Statistics (Panel A, Company A)**

Plant Number	Task Significance	Conflict Resolution	Team Cohesion
Plant A1 (Engine)	2.79 (0.70)	3.94 (0.24)	3.83 (0.79)
Plant A2 (Engine)	2.30 (0.42)	2.88 (0.88)	2.17 (0.24)
Plant A3 (Transmission)	2.57 (0.83)	3.82 (0.45)	2.83 (1.24)
Plant A4 (Foundry)	2.70 (0.92)	3.75 (.)*	3.67 (0.47)
Plant A5 (Stamping)	3.00 (0.73)	4.50 (0.00)	4.67 (0.00)
Plant A6 (Components)	4.35 (0.75)	4.46 (0.51)	4.42 (0.39)
Plant A7 (Components)	3.44 (0.48)	3.78 (0.63)	3.78 (0.69)
Plant A8 (Components)	3.67 (0.49)	4.31 (0.75)	4.08 (0.83)
Plant A9 (Components)	4.25 (0.12)	4.38 (0.18)	4.67 (0.47)
All Plants Median:	**3.00 [1.32]**	**3.94 [0.65]**	**3.83 [1.29]**
All Plants Average:	**3.23 (0.74)**	**3.98 (0.51)**	**3.79 (0.84)**

Table 5.3. **Components of Team Process for ABC Development Teams, Descriptive Statistics (Panel B, Company B)**

Plant Number	Task Significance	Conflict Resolution	Team Cohesion
Plant B1 (Engine)	3.42 (0.56)	3.72 (0.52)	3.89 (0.58)
Plant B2 (Engine)	3.93 (0.61)	4.15 (0.38)	4.27 (0.55)
Plant B3 (Transmission)	3.58 (1.00)	4.00 (0.59)	3.87 (0.69)
Plant B4 (Foundry)	2.42 (0.12)	4.00 (.)*	4.00 (.)*
Plant B5 (Stamping)	2.90 (1.27)	3.00 (1.41)	3.17 (1.18)
Plant B6 (Components)	3.57 (0.33)	3.62 (0.18)	3.83 (0.24)
Plant B7 (Components)	3.79 (0.16)	4.19 (0.24)	4.25 (0.32)
Plant B8 (Components)	3.42 (0.12)	4.00 (0.00)	4.00 (0.00)
Plant B9 (Components)	3.56 (0.10)	4.50 (0.35)	4.11 (1.02)
All Plants Median:	**3.56 [0.52]**	**4.00 [0.50]**	**4.00 [0.33]**
All Plants Average:	**3.40 (0.46)**	**3.91 (0.43)**	**3.93 (0.33)**

*Because of missing items, only one respondent is represented; ( ) standard deviations; [ ] interquartile range

Table 5.4. Inter-rater Reliability Coefficients (Panel A, Company A)

Plant Number	Task Significance	Conflict Resolution	Team Cohesion
Plant A1 (Engine)	0.76	0.97	0.69
Plant A2 (Engine)	0.91	0.61	0.97
Plant A3 (Transmission)	0.66	0.90	0.23
Plant A4 (Foundry)	0.58	0.91	0.89
Plant A5 (Stamping)	0.73	1.00	1.00
Plant A6(Components)	0.72	0.87	0.92
Plant A7 (Components)	0.88	0.78	0.76
Plant A8 (Components)	0.88	0.72	0.66
Plant A9 (Components)	0.99	0.98	0.89

Table 5.4. Inter-rater Reliability Coefficients (Panel B, Company B)

Plant Number	Task Significance	Conflict Resolution	Team Cohesion
Plant B1 (Engine)	0.84	0.88	0.83
Plant B2 (Engine)	0.81	0.93	0.85
Plant B3 (Transmission)	0.50	0.83	0.76
Plant B4 (Foundry)	0.99	1.00	1.00
Plant B5 (Stamping)	0.19	0.00	0.30
Plant B6 (Components)	0.95	0.99	0.97
Plant B7 (Components)	0.99	0.97	0.95
Plant B8 (Components)	0.99	1.00	1.00
Plant B9 (Components)	1.00	0.96	0.48

3.8 Outcome Variables

3.8.1 Model Complexity

The ABC models developed were structured around (a) *the number of activity centers*, (b) the *number of first stage cost drivers*, and (b) the *number of second stage cost drivers*. All data reported were measured using the *ABC Model Questionnaire*. See Table 5.5, Panel A and Panel B.

3.8.2 Number of Activity Centers

The average total number of activity centers for Company A was 25. In Company B, the average number of activity centers in each plant was 41. See Table 5.5, Panel A and Panel B, Column 2.

3.8.3 Number of 1st and 2nd Stage Cost Drivers

Company A used an average of 27.9, 1st stage cost drivers. In contrast, Company B averaged 64.8 first stage drivers. A similar pattern is evidenced with 16.7, second stage cost drivers for Company A and 21.9 for Company B. See Table 5.5, Panels A and B, Columns 3 and 4.,

Overall model complexity was defined as the sum of activity centers, first stage cost drivers and second stage cost drivers for each plant. The raw data were standardized before being combined (*Z*-scores are reported in Table 5.5, Column 5).[15]

3.8.4 Time to Develop the Initial ABC Model

The time to develop the initial ABC model was calculated as the difference between when ABC training began to when the first product costs were generated.[16] Company A's teams averaged 7.9 months versus 8 months for Company B's teams. See Table 5.5, column 6.

4. RESULTS

To test the expectations, Partial Least Squares (PLS) was used to perform path-analytic modeling. PLS evaluates the measurement and structural parameters of a causal model in an iterative fashion using ordinary least squares regressions. By working with one construct and a subset of measures related to that construct or adjacent constructs, complex models are separated (Barclay, Higgins and Thompson, 1995).

Table 5.5. Characteristics of ABC Models Developed, Descriptive Statistics (Panel A, Company A)

Plant Number	Number of Activity Centers	Number of 1st Stage Cost Drivers	Number of 2nd Stage Cost Drivers	ABC Model Complexity (Z-Scores)	Model Development Time (Months)
Plant A1 (Engine)	13	20	4	-3.67	8
Plant A2 (Engine)	29	80	39	2.55	12
Plant A3 (Transmission)	10	16	7	-3.80	12
Plant A4 (Foundry)	31	26	9	-1.75	10
Plant A5 (Stamping)	13	23	14	-2.76	4
Plant A6 (Components)	21	11	6	-3.28	4
Plant A7 (Components)	47	8	6	-1.53	9
Plant A8 (Components)	23	25	39	0.04	8
Plant A9 (Components)	42	42	26	1.00	4
All Plants Median:	**23**	**23**	**9**	**-1.75**	**8.0**
All Plants Average:	**25.4**	**27.9**	**16.7**	**-1.47**	**7.9**

Table 5.5. Characteristics of ABC Models Developed, Descriptive Statistics (Panel B, Company B)

Plant Number	Number of Activity Centers	Number of 1st Stage Cost Drivers	Number of 2nd Stage Cost Drivers	ABC Model Complexity (Z-scores)	Model Development Time (Months)
Plant B1 (Engine)	40	53	21	0.87	5
Plant B2 (Engine)	21	38	10	-1.94	10
Plant B3 (Transmission)	51	77	19	2.41	10
Plant B4 (Foundry)	32	54	13	-0.30	8
Plant B5 (Stamping)	53	53	22	1.88	7
Plant B6 (Components)	47	74	36	3.37	7
Plant B7 (Components)	35	72	14	0.67	9
Plant B8 (Components)	43	82	20	2.10	8
Plant B9 (Components)	48	80	42	4.15	8
All Plants Median:	**43**	**72**	**20**	**1.88**	**8.0**
All Plants Average:	**41.1**	**64.8**	**21.9**	**1.47**	**8.0**

This segmenting procedure makes PLS suitable for small sample sizes.[17] The model's path coefficients are standardized βs, which are interpreted in the same manner as β weights in OLS regression (Hulland, 1998). Bootstrapping provides a means to evaluate the empirical sampling distribution of parameter estimates (Efron and Tibshirani 1993). Bootstrapping (1,000 samples with replacement) was used to assess the statistical significance of the path coefficients.

4.1 Tests of Research Expectations

In this section the tests of expectations are reported. Table 5.6 provides a Pearson, product-moment correlation matrix across variables. Results are shown in Table 5.7 and the coefficients are superimposed on the path diagram in Figure 5.2 for ease of interpretation.

The first set of expectations relates to determinants of conflict resolution. In expectation 1 we posit that the ability to resolve conflicts to decrease as ABC team size increases. The link was marginally supported ($p < 0.10$) but in the opposite direction to that predicted. Similarly, Expectation 2 predicts that as team heterogeneity increases, the team's ability to resolve conflicts decreases. No support was found for this relation. We also hypothesize that the presence of an external consultant is positively associated with the team's ability to resolve conflicts (Expectation 3). Results indicate no support was found for this association. Theory predicts that conflict resolution is an important determinant of project team performance where tasks are difficult and outcomes are ambiguously defined. We sought to identify antecedents of team conflict resolution skills that would have managerial implications for the selection and composition of ABC teams. However, we were not successful and surmise that conflict resolution skills are likely the product of personality factors that were not measured. This suggests that team formation and the resulting "chemistry" of team members are not easily achieved by "cookbook" formulae employing optimal team size or skill mix.

The second set of expectations predicted that as the level of competition increases managers would increase ABC training (Expectation 4) and team size (Expectation 5). Results show no support for either of these expectations. While we find these results surprising, it could be the case that both Core and Non Core plants allocated similar resources due to plant staffing constraints.

The next set of expectations focused on variables affecting task significance. Beginning with Expectation 6 we predicted a positive relation between increased levels of ABC training and the perceived level of task significance. This expectation was strongly supported in the predicted direction ($p < 0.01$).

Table 5.6. **Correlation Matrix**

	1	2	3	4	5	6	7	8	9	10
1. ABC Training		.351	.352	-.225	.248	.628	.417	.479	-.171	-.044
2. Team Size	.216		.478	.129	.140	.581	.280	.308	-.219	.008
3. Heterogeneity	.291	.625*		.203	-.238	.317	.230	.390	-.200	-.262
4. Consultant	-.107	.189	.172		.000	.139	-.086	.086	.546	-.022
5. Competition	.214	-.002	-.282	.000		.636	.400	.399	.302	-.318
6. Task Significance	.547*	.535*	.260	.144	.672*		.570	.696	.091	-.347
7. Conflict Resolution	.314	.370	.283	-.077	.423	.595*		.883	-.193	-.349
8. Team Cohesion	.331	.345	.391	.117	.418	.696*	.857*		-.103	-.560
9. Model Complexity	-.160	-.155	-.227	.603*	.299	.114	-.264	-.139		-.039
10. Development Time	-.017	-.198	-.331	.023	-.304	-.497*	-.446*	-.695*	.036	

Note. * significant at $p < .05$, 2-tailed.
Pearson product-moment correlations are below the diagonal. Spearman rank-order correlations are above the diagonal.

Table 5.7. **Results of PLS: Hypothesis Testing, Path Coefficients (t-statistics in parentheses)**

		Path to:						
		ABC Training	Team Size	Conflict Resolution	Task Significance	Team Cohesion	Model Complexity	Development Time
Adjusted R^2:		0.00	0.00	0.17	0.62	0.79	0.60	0.48
Path From:	**Predicted Sign**							
1. Competition	+,+	0.214 (0.838)	-0.002 (-0.010)		0.582** (4.602)		0.477** (2.896)	
2. Team Size	-			0.337* (1.413)				
3. Heterogeneity	-			0.101 (0.457)				
4. Consultant	+,+			-0.159 (0.671)			0.570** (3.564)	
5. ABC Training	+				0.422** (2.273)			
6. Task Significance	+					0.287* (1.747)		
7. Conflict Resolution	+,-					0.686** (4.003)	-0.421* (1.611)	
8. Team Cohesion	-							-0.703** (3.838)
9. Model Complexity	+							-0.061 (0.360)

Note. * significant at $p < .10$, 1-tailed.
     ** significant at $p < .05$, 1-tailed.
     $N = 18$.

106

Figure 5.2. Tests of Research Expectations: Path Coefficients

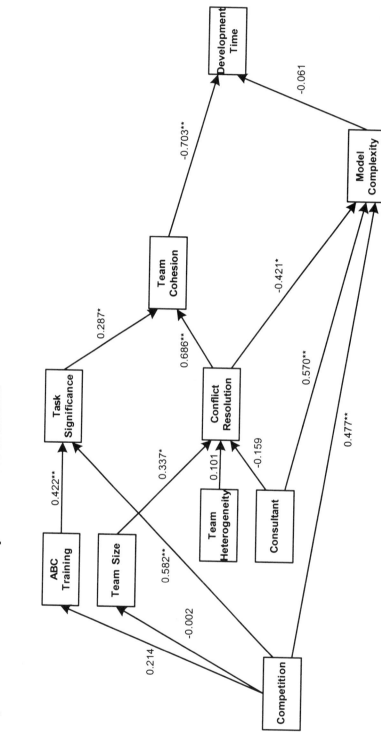

Note.
* significant at *p* < .10
** significant at *p* < .05

Expectation 7 predicted that ABC Teams facing a high level of competition will experience a higher level of task significance than ABC teams that face a low level of competition. This expectation also was strongly supported ($p < 0.01$).

Following this, we hypothesize that as the level of perceived task significance increases, so does the level of team cohesion (expectation 8). This expectation was marginally supported ($p < 0.10$). Another determinant of team cohesion was conflict resolution. In Expectation 9 we expect that as the team's ability to resolve conflicts increases so would the level of team cohesion. This expectation is strongly supported ($p < 0.01$)

Three variables are hypothesized to explain ABC model complexity. First, Expectation 10 predicts that as the team's ability to resolve conflicts increases, ABC model complexity decreases. We find marginal support for this expectation ($p < 0101$). Next, we posited that as the perceived level of competition increases, ABC model complexity increases (expectation 11). Strong support is found for this expectation ($p < 0.01$). Finally, with expectation 12 we predict a positive association between using a low cost strategy and ABC model complexity. Results show support for this expectation ($p < 0.01$).

In our last set of expectations, we linked model development time to the level of team cohesion (expectation 13) and model complexity (14). We suggested that as the level of team cohesion increased, the time to develop the initial ABC model would decrease. Strong support was found for this expectation ($p < 0.01$). No support, however, is found for the relation between an increase in model complexity and an increase in initial ABC model development time.

5. SUMMARY

In this chapter we examine the ABC development process in 18 plants of our two automobile manufacturers. From our model, we test 14 expectations using PLS. The first series of relations linked the team input variables of team size, team heterogeneity and the presence of an external consultant to conflict resolution. We find a marginally significant relation between team and conflict resolution, but the direction of the effect is not as predicted — as team size increases, the ability to resolve conflicts increases. One explanation is that since many of the teams were relatively homogeneous, consisting of people from the finance staff, they all held similar views about the task and thus were able to resolve conflicts more expediently. We also expected a positive relation between having an external consultant as part of the team process and the level of conflict resolution but found none.

We hypothesized, but found no support for, a relationship between competition and the amount of ABC training and team size. The lack of support for these expectations is surprising, however, it could be the case that resources were so limited across all plants that no difference is observed.

We discovered that the level of ABC training and the degree of competition affected task significance. In turn, task significance and the ability to resolve conflicts influenced team cohesion which ultimately was the major explanator of time to develop the first ABC model. We discuss this further below. The implications of these findings are that ABC training has the obvious benefit of providing technical knowledge, but also influences how team members see the ABC model development. Competition plays a similar role in affecting perceptions of the significance of the task at hand.

Two of the three factors we hypothesize would influence ABC model complexity are found to be significant. First, while we predicted a positive association between the presence of an ABC consultant and model complexity, we found that the presence of the consultant in Company B led to the creation of more complex models. This is probably a result of Company's B strategy of being a low cost producer and a corresponding need for more detailed cost information made possible by a complex ABC model. We also find support for the relation between the degree of competition and model complexity. As teams experience greater competition the need to focus on developing accurate product costs increases.[18] Greater accuracy in product costs is often achieved with greater complexity.

As mentioned earlier, the most significant predictor of time to develop the first ABC model is team cohesion. Team cohesion is the key factor for local management to consider when developing ABC teams. As has been true for years, fostering a work environment in which desired behaviors can flourish is probably the most difficult management task.

While we also predicted that increased model complexity would lead to greater time to develop the first ABC model, no relation was found. Since what constitutes complexity with ABC models is itself a difficult task, much more research has to be accomplished before clearer relations can be established. We do surmise, however, that the time it takes to develop more complex models is relatively small once the initial model design is completed.

Previous discussions on ABC have suggested that ABC models can be successfully implemented by a team of heterogeneous, skilled employees, trained in cost system design and provided them with adequate computing resources. In short, the focus has been on providing the right mix of inputs to cost system design. In this chapter we have attempted to shed light on how inputs influence team dynamics which in turn are related to cost system design decisions and the speed of project completion.

NOTES

[1] Jim Hesford coauthored this chapter with us. We gratefully acknowledge his contribution.

[2] See Lewin (1943); Shields, (1995); Foster and Swenson (1997) and Anderson, (1995).

[3] The construct that we are investigating in this paper is "conflict resolution" and not the level of "conflict" per se. When respondents are asked about conflict resolution, their experiences with conflict in a group are impounded in their answers to the questions (see Thomas, 1976).

[4] In this study, team heterogeneity is measured as the number of functional areas (such as manufacturing, engineering, etc.) represented.

[5] We do not explicitly model the link between team size and heterogeneity. While our measure of heterogeneity relates to greater representation of different functional areas, some teams may have a disproportionate number of team members from one functional area, while others may be comprised of an even distribution of members from several areas.

[6] In this context our observation was that task significance was a process rather than input variable. For instance, some ABC members were drafted into the ABC implementation while others volunteered. Some team members understood the importance of building an ABC model in an expedient fashion, whereas others understood the task's significance when they became educated about the benefits of ABC. Thus, task significance is not considered a fixed input here but rather a variable that is more related to team processes and training.

[7] ABC team members received various types of training including formal course work, in-house seminars and meetings sponsored by the Corporate ABC group.

[8] While task significance is usually a task-related variable, we group the construct together with the team dynamic's variables. We hypothesize that management innovations are more likely to fail if a project team does not see what they are doing as highly important for their organization. The task significance measure in this paper is a group measure and, in part, captures members' motivation to perform as a team.

[9] In our model, Figure 5.1, the perceived level of competition is the factor we model as the one representing the external environment. We chose this factor as representative of the external environment for two reasons. First, discussions with many plant employees and ABC team members indicated that felt competition was the external factor that drove behavior in their organizations. Second, we chose only one factor for the sake of developing a parsimonious model.

---

[10] An activity dictionary defines admissible "activities" that are cost objects in the 1st of a two-stage cost assignment.

[11] We note that this expectation is specific to our organizational context and may not hold in situations where consultants are not faced with the goal of being the low cost producer.

[12] Some of the descriptive statistics related to the ABC teams was also reported earlier in Chapter 4. We reprint it here mainly for convenience.

[13] The results of the analysis are qualitatively unchanged when a measure of "perceived effectiveness of the consultant" is substituted for those plants that use consultants.

[14] Subject to data limitations, we performed a confirmatory factor analysis on individual team member responses ($N = 89$). Although our sample size was below minimum recommended levels and was multivariate nonnormal, none of the correlations among the three latent variables included the value of 1.0. Combined with face validity of the items and satisfactory measures of reliability, the analyses are supportive of scale validity.

[15] One outlier was dropped.

[16] Training time is included because aspects of ABC design (e.g., defining activity centers) are often started during training.

[17] Fornell and Bookstein (1982b) note that meaningful PLS analyses can sometimes have a sample size smaller than the number of variables. Chin and Newsted (1999) describe an extreme case of a model with 21 latent variables, 672 indicators and a sample size of 20. The literature says little about sample size requirements, but estimates range from 5 cases per predictor (Tabachnick and Fidell, 1989) to formulas such as $N > 50 + m$ (Harris, 1975), or a specific number such as 100 (Nunnally, 1978). Such recommendations are driven by unstated assumptions of effect size and statistical power (Algina and Olejnik, 2000). For this study, a 2 (3) predictor regression will be able to detect, with a power of 0.8, an effect whose R^2 is 0.35 (0.38).

[18] While we were in the field, we experienced strike activity, first hand, due to the threat of outsourcing at some of the component's plants. Outside competition is a very real threat to some plants in the automobile industry, and it is becoming much more of a concern to plants whose technology and products are being threatened by both domestic and foreign competition.

Chapter 6

EVALUATING ABC PROJECTS: SPONSORS, GATEKEEPERS, ENABLERS, AND IMPEDIMENTS

1. OVERVIEW

In Chapters 4 and 5 we focused on the ABC design team and how team dynamics affect project outcomes and are affected by external circumstances. In this chapter we decrease the magnification of our microscope to get a broader view of ABC implementation while retaining our focus on specific ABC implementation projects. Specifically, we address the question of which organizational and technical factors affect outcomes of ABC implementation projects. Historically, ABC implementation studies have focused on "fixing" traditional cost systems' distorted product costs by using causally related "cost drivers" to assign overhead costs. Later studies argued that a judiciously designed ABC system could also be an effective tool for modifying employee behavior to support corporate strategy.[1] Since then, evidence of ABC implementation failures[2] has caused researchers to suggest that achieving either objective depends critically on certain organizational and technical factors. Research[3] supports this; however, as discussed in Chapter 2, these studies focus on a firm's overall experience with ABC rather than on specific ABC implementation projects.

Although we employed a mix of objective and subjective performance measures of the ABC project in Chapter 5, like previous survey research that studies ABC implementation almost exclusively from the perspective of finance managers, there is always a concern that a broader survey of organizational participants would reveal different assessments of project success. We must guard against the possibility that ABC team members are "too close" to the project to understand its relation to the organization or that, lacking a managerial perspective, they are unable to fully comprehend the implications of ABC for the organization. Consequently, in this chapter, we broaden our inquiry to study the ABC implementation process using survey data from both the management team at the ABC implementation site and ABC design team members. In chapter 7 we explore multiple dimensions of ABC project effectiveness and examine whether there are differences between the way that managers and ABC team members think about these issues and whether these opinions change as the ABC system matures.

To structure our analysis, we begin with a theoretical model of organizational change (Rogers, 1962; 1983) that relates conditions in the external environment to ABC project management and to project outcomes. We use survey data and a statistical analysis method known as structural equation modeling to explore the descriptive validity of the model. We find that our data are consistent with the proposed model. Variables related to environmental conditions that directly influence evaluations of the ABC system are: the quality of other information systems; and, the extent to which superior individual performance is believed to be recognized and rewarded at the site. Variables related to ABC project management that directly influence overall evaluations of the ABC system are: whether top (firm-level) managers and the local labor union are believed to have supported the implementation project and whether adequate resources were dedicated to the project. Although the analysis identifies correlates of local managers' involvement in the ABC implementation project, in contrast to previous studies we find no evidence that involvement of local managers influences evaluations of ABC systems directly or indirectly. In summary, our analysis provides the first evidence of a structured relationship between environmental conditions, ABC project management and evaluations of the resulting ABC system.

2. DETERMINANTS OF ABC PROJECT OUTCOMES

The basic model of organizational change that we use as the point of departure for our analysis is depicted in Figure 6.1. The general model relates conditions in the external environment to how the firm manages change and whether the change is successfully enacted (Rogers 1962). In Rogers' model, managers' consideration of an innovation is motivated or constrained by circumstances in the firm's external and internal environment and by characteristics of the individual evaluating the innovation--- what we refer to collectively as *environmental conditions*. Subsequent evaluations of the innovation are influenced by comparison between the innovation, the status quo, and alternative innovations, and by factors related to the innovation experience--- what we term *ABC project management* factors. Rogers conducted a comprehensive review of hundreds of research studies on organizational change and concluded that the framework is robust to the nature of organizational change and the institutional setting in which change occurs. Particular environmental conditions that merit consideration are dependent on the nature of the organizational change. We base our selection of variables for consideration on prior research on ABC implementation and, more generally, information technology implementation. We also consult practitioner accounts of ABC implementation projects to identify other factors that may have influenced project outcomes. Variables associated with the particular change management project --- in this case, ABC implementation --- were derived from the literature on project teams that was discussed in Chapter 4 and 5.

Table 3.1 summarized factors that we identified from prior research and practitioner accounts as influential in ABC implementation. Table 6.1 separates these factors into those that can be considered to reflect external environmental conditions as opposed to decisions related to ABC project management. We should note that when we use the term, "external" to describe environmental conditions, we are referring to forces that are external to the ABC implementation project but which are hypothesized to impinge upon the project. Among external environmental conditions, we distinguish characteristics of the organization in which the project is located from characteristics of people employed by the organization.

The rightmost column of Table 6.1 indicates how our research incorporates these variables in the analysis of ABC implementation. In some cases a variable name indicates that a particular factor is included in the analysis of this chapter. An entry of, "*GM vs C*" means that the "variable" does not vary within the firms of our study, but does vary between the firms of our study. We do not measure these variables directly; however, any differences that we discover in the degree to which the model fits each firm may be caused in part by these factors. Another entry, the word "*Team*", indicates that a factor is part of the analysis of Chapters 4 and 5. This distinction points to one problem with the Rogers model, namely the tendency to blur the distinction between events within the change management project and organizational outcomes of the change management project. The problem has an inherently hierarchical structure: team members are imbedded within ABC development teams; ABC development teams and management teams are imbedded within ABC implementation sites; and ABC implementation sites are imbedded within firms. Where previous research has ignored the hierarchical nature of ABC implementation by using a single point estimate (e.g., one survey response) to describe a firm's ABC initiative, we attempt to present a richer picture of ABC implementation. We do this by studying separately the ABC team process and the relation of the team to organizational outcomes. In the case of the technological factor of system compatibility, the rightmost column of Table 6.1 indicates that the variable is not applicable in this study. Although Anderson (1995) found that assessments of system compatibility were important in the firm's decision to adopt ABC, all of the ABC projects of this study developed stand-alone, PC-based ABC models. Thus, compatibility with existing systems was not a

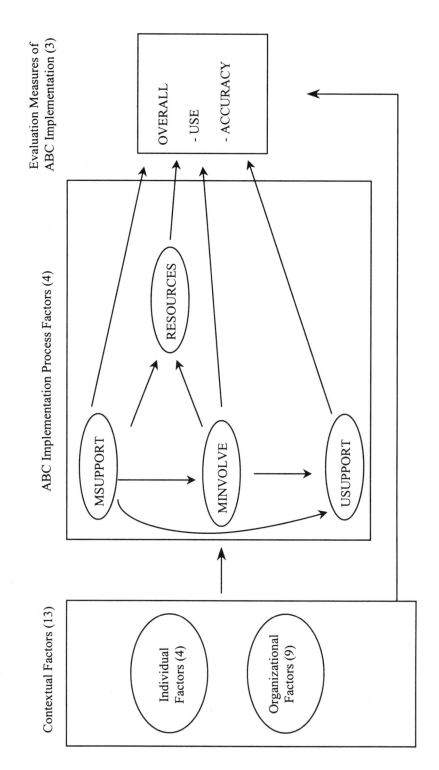

Figure 6.1. **Structural Model of ABC Implementation**

Table 6.1. Candidate Variables for Analysis of Determinants of ABC Implementation Outcomes: Conditions of the External Environment versus ABC Project Management

CANDIDATE VARIABLE	Environmental Conditions		ABC Project Management & Team Process	Variable Name in Subsequent Analysis (*)
	Individual Factors	Organizational Factors		
Individual Characteristics				
Disposition toward change	X		X	CHANGE
Production Process Knowledge	X		X	*Team*
Role Involvement	X		X	COMMIT & VALUES
Adequate ABC training	X			*M vs. D*
Organizational Factors				
Centralization		X		*GM vs C*
Functional specialization		X		*GM vs C*
Formalization/ job standardization		X	X	*GM vs C*
Vertical Differentiation		X		*GM vs C*
Formal Support in Accounting Dept.			X	*GM vs C*
Support			X	
- Top Management				MSUPPORT,
- Local management				MINVOLVE,
- Local union				USUPPORT
Internal communications		X	X	*GM vs. C*
Extrinsic reward systems		X	X	REWARD
ABC Training investments			X	*Team*
Technological Factors				
Complexity for users			X	*Team*
Compatibility with existing systems		X		*Not applicable*
Relative improvement over existing system (accuracy and timeliness)		X		INFOQUAL
Relevance to managers' decisions and compatibility with firm strategy		X	X	IMPCOST
Task Characteristics				
Uncertainty / lack of goal clarity			*X*	*Team*
Variety			*X*	*Team*
Worker autonomy			*X*	*Team*
Worker responsibility			*X*	*Team*
Resource Adequacy			*X*	*Team*
Availability of ABC software			*X*	*Team*

Table 6.1. (continued) **Candidate Variables for Analysis of Determinants of ABC Implementation Outcomes: Conditions of the External Environment versus ABC Project Management**

CANDIDATE VARIABLE	Environmental Conditions		ABC Project Management & Team Process	Variable Name in Subsequent Analysis (*)
	Individual Factors	Organizational Factors		
External Environment				
Heterogeneity of demands		X		TURB
Competition		X		COMPETE
Environmental uncertainty		X		
- Likelihood of layoffs				LAYOFF,
- Growth opportunities				NOGROW,
- Labor relations				LABOR
- Importance of site to firm				IMPPLT
External Communications/ external experts		X	X	*GM vs. C and Team*
* *Legend:* GM vs. C indicates variable that differs between but not within companies. M. vs. D. indicates a variable that differs between managers and ABC developers but not within each group. Team indicates a variable that reflects processes within the ABC development team and which is considered in Chapters 5 and 6. The designation, "not applicable" indicates a variable that did not vary for the ABC sites in this study and thus is not open to investigation.				

defining factor in the success of the ABC project. However, as we discuss in Chapter 9, it became an issue several years later.

Three related research questions are considered in this chapter. Specifically, what are the associations among:

1. evaluations of ABC systems and contextual variables that represent individual and organizational circumstances.

2. evaluations of ABC systems and ABC project management.

3. local managers' involvement in the ABC implementation process and contextual variables that represent individual and organizational circumstances.

These research questions are depicted in Figure 6.1 as arrows between three groups of variables: environmental factors, ABC project management factors and ABC implementation outcomes. Discussion of specific variables and relationships between process variables follows.

3. IDENTIFICATION AND MEASUREMENT OF VARIABLES[4]

3.1 Measure of ABC Project Outcomes

The analysis of this chapter uses a single, overall measure of ABC implementation success (OVERALL). In our surveys, we ask informants to weigh the costs and benefits of ABC implementation, and judge whether in their experience, ABC has proven valuable. We defer discussion and analysis of two other measures of ABC implementation outcomes (ACCURACY and USE) for Chapter 7.

3.2 Environmental Condition Variables

Rogers' (1962; 1983) model of organizational change suggests two categories of variables that influence innovation decisions: attributes of the decision-maker, and characteristics of the organization in relation to the external environment. For the research sites, the external environment includes both market forces and influences of the firm and other sites. To explore research question 1 we examine the significance of direct associations between environmental factors described below and evaluations of the ABC system.

Four factors that may influence the individual decision-maker are considered: 1) the extent to which they believe that change is warranted (CHANGE)--- what the organizational psychology literature terms "felt need for change"; 2) individual commitment to the organization and the plant (COMMIT); 3) the extent to which the individual identifies with the values of the organization and the plant (VALUES); and, 4) the extent to which individual performance is linked to rewards (REWARD). It is important to note that REWARD does *not* measure the extent to which individuals believe that they will be rewarded if they implement ABC or use ABC data. There was no evidence of explicit changes to management control practices or incentives aimed at promoting ABC use. Consequently, we assess the impact of reward expectancy on managers' evaluation of the ABC system and motivation to become involved in the ABC project.

Seven aspects of the site environment that may affect managers' willingness to engage in ABC implementation or evaluation of the ABC system are examined: 1) the competitive environment (COMPETE); 2) the quality of existing information systems (INFOQUAL); 3) environmental turbulence (TURB); 4) the likelihood of employee layoffs (LAYOFF); 5) impediments to plant growth (NOGROW); 6) the perceived importance of the plant to the company (IMPPLT); and 7) the perceived importance of cost reduction to the plant (IMPCOST). Advocates of ABC claim that new cost data are most valuable when heightened competition or limited growth prospects cause firms to focus on cost reduction. The measures, COMPETE, NOGROW and IMPCOST measure these motivations for adopting ABC. Even in firms that face heightened competition, some operations are less threatened than others. The decision to include 'core' and peripheral component plants in this study was an attempt to maximize the range of competitive threat experienced by sites of a single firm. The perceived importance of the plant (IMPPLT) to the company is included as a potential mitigating factor to external competition.

Sites from a firm often have diverse historical origins that are reflected in local "legacy" information systems that are more or less effective in meeting managers' information needs. Kwon and Zmud (1987) argue that adoption of new information technology depends critically upon fit with and incremental improvement upon existing systems. A measure of respondents' beliefs about the quality of existing information systems (INFOQUAL) is used to examine how the current information environment influences managers' commitment to or evaluation of the ABC system. Organizational theorists argue that there are limits to the amount of change that an organization can absorb effectively. We heard countless stories of "programs of the month" (at times in reference to ABC) during our interviews. Thus we include a measure of plant-level turbulence (TURB) as a likely impediment to ABC implementation.

Finally, cost reduction efforts often produce reductions in employment. In a unionized environment with contractual employment guarantees, managers are often reluctant or unable to engage in protracted negotiations that are necessary to reduce employment. As a result, many of the prospective benefits of ABC systems may be unrealizable. A measure of the likelihood of layoffs (LAYOFF) is used to capture this potential deterrent to ABC implementation. In the same vein, the quality of historical management-labor relations (LABOR) is included as a possible precursor to union support of the ABC project.

3.3 ABC Project Management Variables Related to ABC Implementation

Appropriate process variables for analysis and the relation between process variables depend upon firm-specific ABC implementation strategies. Previous studies that consider the relation between process variables and ABC project outcomes test for correlation between a wide range of possible process variables without knowledge *ex ante* of firms' implementation processes. As a result, tests that pool firms with different implementation strategies do not distinguished between the case of a process variable being irrelevant and the case where a process is employed but does not influence ABC project outcomes. Prior to developing the survey instruments, we interviewed the firms' corporate ABC managers and reviewed corporate training manuals to develop a description of the ABC implementation process. This process and the variable measures intended to capture each component are described below.

The general structure of GM and Chrysler's ABC implementation process is depicted inside of the box labeled 'ABC Project Management Variables' in Figure 6.1. Specifically, firm-level managers committed the company to ABC implementation prior to the initiation of an ABC project at the research sites. Respondents' opinions about the strength of this commitment are measured by the variable, MSUPPORT. The management awareness sessions that each firm used to introduce ABC to local managers was intended to increase managers' knowledge of ABC and to secure their involvement in the project. Respondents' beliefs about whether local commitment was achieved are measured by the variable, MINVOLVE. The proposed relation between MSUPPORT and MINVOLVE reflects the direction of influence described above. Both firms assigned responsibility for implementing ABC to local management. Although corporate resources were available to augment or support the team, team members were selected and freed from other responsibilities (or not) by local managers. Local managers were also given discretion in the decision to involve local union leaders in the project. The adequacy of resources committed to the ABC project is measured with the variable, RESOURCES. The degree to which the union was aware of and involved in the ABC project is measured by the variable,

USUPPORT. The proposed relation between MINVOLVE and both RESOURCES and USUPPORT reflects the gatekeeper role that local managers are assigned. The proposed relation between MSUPPORT and USUPPORT reflects a possible flow of influence from top managers of the firm, to the local union. Although top managers did not intervene directly in local union affairs, at least one firm noted that the firm's decision to implement ABC had become a negotiating point with labor at the national level. The proposed relation between MSUPPORT and RESOURCES reflects the support that the corporate ABC group provided development teams after local management initiated an ABC project.

The relationships described above reflect firm-specific implementation processes that have been ignored in previous research. However, finding that these relations hold is simply evidence of face validity of the data rather than evidence on the proposed research questions. To explore research question 2 we examine the effects of each process variable on evaluations of the ABC system. Because implementation of ABC is a local management decision, we explore research question 3 by examining the association between environmental factors and local managers' involvement in the ABC project (MINVOLVE). We also consider the role of the environmental factor, historical labor relations (LABOR), on union support of the ABC project.

4. DATA ANALYSIS

4.1 Descriptive Statistics

Responses to 61 survey questions are used to measure the 19 variables associated with environmental conditions, project management factors and project outcomes. Table 6.2 provides the full text of the survey questions developed for each latent variable, as well as summary descriptive statistics and Cronbach's (1951) measure of construct validity. Responses to 58 of the survey items generated responses that span the five-point, Likert-type scale. With two exceptions the constructs are adequately identified, with Cronbach's alpha exceeding the 0.6 level used in exploratory research. Item-level response rates from the 265 respondents ranges from 190 to 265. There are typically two reasons non-response: 1) inadequate knowledge for forming an assessment, and 2) apprehension about respondent anonymity. Understandably, items that generated the highest non-response were those related to management-union relations, a politically sensitive topic.

Table 6.2. Descriptive Statistics for Survey Items Used to Measure Variables (Panel A)

Latent Construct	Survey Items (R= reverse coded item); 5= strongly agree, 1=strongly disagree	Item N	Item Mean	Std. Dev.	Cronbach's Std. Alpha
MEASURES OF ABC IMPLEMENTATION SUCCESS					
OVERALL: Overall Value of ABC					.93
1	Despite the implementation challenges, I am convinced that ABC is the right tool for helping us manage costs in this company.	245	3.8	.75	
2	Overall, the benefits of ABC data outweigh the costs of installing a new system.	220	3.6	.87	
3	Supporting ABC is the right thing to do in this company.	240	3.9	.79	
4	If I were asked to decide whether this company should continue implementing ABC, I would vote to continue.	240	3.9	.92	
5	In general ABC is a good thing for this company.	244	4.0	.70	
ACCURACY: Perceived Accuracy of ABC data					.65
1 (R)	The ABC costs do not seem reasonable to me based on what I know about this plant.	233	3.8	.81	
2	The results from the ABC model matched my intuition about costs of production.	223	3.6	.77	
3	Data from the ABC model provides an accurate assessment of costs in this plant.	240	3.7	.72	
USE: Perceived Use of ABC data					.70
1	Information from the ABC model has had a noticeable positive impact on this plant.	228	2.9	.83	
2 (R)	I am reluctant to use ABC data in place of costs from the traditional cost system.	232	3.4	.96	
3 (R)	The ABC model has not been used and has been 'gathering dust' since it was completed.	233	3.5	.97	
4	Data from the ABC model are used for special cost studies.	229	3.2	1.0	
ABC IMPLEMENTATION PROCESS VARIABLES					
MSUPPORT: Top Management Support					.77
1	This company's top managers have provided visible support for the ABC initiative.	252	3.4	1.1	
2	Support for implementing ABC in this company comes from both the manufacturing operations and finance groups.	254	3.2	1.0	
3	Support for implementing ABC in this company is widespread.	250	2.9	1.0	
MINVOLVE: Local Management Knowledge of and Involvement in ABC					.72
1	The managers of this plant are knowledgeable about the theory of ABC.	243	3.4	.80	
2	Most managers of this plant are capable of using ABC data to reduce costs.	238	3.1	1.0	
3	Most managers of the plant were involved in determining how their departmental expenses were allocated to activities and products.	228	3.5	1.0	
4	When the developers of the ABC model met with local managers, they received suggestions from the managers.	205	3.4	.91	
USUPPORT: Union Support					.77
1	The local union is receptive to the concept of ABC.	190	2.9	.87	
2	The local union was involved in decisions that affected the ABC model.	192	2.6	.99	

Table 6.2. (continued) Descriptive Statistics for Survey Items Used to Measure Variables (Panel B)

Latent Construct	Survey Items (R= reverse coded item); 5= strongly agree, 1=strongly disagree	Item N	Item Mean	Std. Dev.	Cronbach's Std. Alpha
RESOURCES: Adequacy of resources for the ABC development project					.63
1	The people who developed the ABC model had the equipment and materials needed to do their job.	214	3.9	.63	
2	The people who developed the ABC model had access to the people from whom they needed to get information.	224	4.0	.60	
3	The ABC development project was adequately staffed to insure completion of the task in time allotted.	210	3.3	.90	
CONTEXTUAL VARIABLES					
COMPETE: Competitive Environment					.54
1	Future demand for the products that this plant produces is uncertain.	264	2.6	1.0	
2	Competitive pressures could cause this plant to close.	264	3.3	1.0	
3	This plant has had a lot of management turnover in recent years.	263	3.3	.98	
4	This plant faces competition from other plants in this company for business.	241	3.3	1.2	
5	This plant faces stiff competition from outside companies for business.	264	3.8	.97	
INFOQUAL: Quality of other information systems					.76
1	Most of the data required for a good ABC model are readily available in this plant.	222	3.0	1.1	
2	The plant's information systems generally provide data that are accurate and up to date.	246	3.0	1.0	
3 (R)	The information systems of this plant contain many data errors.	238	2.8	1.0	
TURB: Environmental Turbulence					.61
1	The working environment at this plant changes constantly.	264	2.9	.88	
2	Manufacturing processes at this plant change all the time.	261	3.0	.96	
3	New management programs are introduced all the time in this plant.	265	3.5	.82	
LAYOFF: History of Employee Layoffs					.70
1 (R)	The threat of layoffs or cutbacks to hourly workers is low.	264	2.4	.99	
2	This plant has had major cutbacks and layoffs in recent years.	264	2.3	1.1	
NOGROW: Impediments to plant growth					.71
1	Getting authorization to hire new employees for this plant is difficult.	263	4.0	.93	
2	We have difficulty getting authorization to hire replacements for employees who retire or leave this plant.	263	3.6	1.1	
LABOR: Quality of labor relations					.87
1	At this plant the union and management have similar goals.	261	2.9	1.1	
2 (R)	Relations between labor and management need to be improved at this plant.	261	2.4	.92	
3	Labor and management in this plant work well together.	262	3.2	.98	

Table 6.2. (continued) Descriptive Statistics for Survey Items Used to Measure Variables (Panel C)

Latent Construct	Survey Items (R= reverse coded item); 5= strongly agree, 1=strongly disagree	Item N	Item Mean	Std. Dev.	Cronbach's Std. Alpha
IMPPLT: Importance of the plant to company					.78
1	This plant is one of the most important manufacturing sites of this company.	241	4.0	.87	
2	This plant produces products that have a major influence on this company's profitability.	264	4.4	.70	
3	This plant is critical for the success of this company.	262	4.0	1.0	
IMPCOST: Importance of cost reduction to plant					.40
1	This plant's cost reduction efforts are important to the company.	264	4.3	.53	
2	Cost reduction is the most important objective in this plant.	264	3.0	.94	
3 (R)	Cost reduction is not a major concern in this plant.	263	4.2	.82	
CHANGE: Felt need for change					.58
1	Changes in the way we work in this plant are needed.	265	3.8	.85	
2 (R)	There is no need for this plant to change the way it does things.	265	4.2	.73	
3	I would like to see changes in plant policies and procedures.	264	3.6	.71	
COMMIT: Commitment to the organization					.73
1	I am proud to work for this company.	264	4.3	.65	
2 (R)	I feel very little loyalty to this company.	264	4.2	1.0	
3	I am proud to work for this plant.	264	4.2	.77	
4 (R)	I feel very little loyalty to this plant.	265	4.1	1.1	
VALUES: Shared organizational values					.75
1	My values and the values of this company are quite similar.	264	3.7	.69	
2	My values and the values at this plant are quite similar.	263	3.6	.82	
REWARD: Reward expectancy					.84
1	In this plant, high quality work increases my chances for a raise, a bonus, or a promotion.	264	3.6	1.0	
2	In this plant, financial rewards are tied directly to performance.	264	3.1	1.0	
3	The ability to reduce costs is rewarded in this plant.	264	3.3	.95	
4	In this plant, high performance is recognized and rewarded.	263	3.3	.92	

The higher response rates for environmental variables, which depend on general plant knowledge alone, relative to ABC project management variables, which require specialized knowledge of the ABC project, suggests that inadequate knowledge may also explain differential response rates.[5]

4.2 Determinants of Overall ABC Implementation Success

4.2.1 Method

Structural equation modeling (SEM) is used to investigate the correspondence of our data with the proposed associations of Figure 6.1. SEM is a method of assessing the correspondence of a proposed set of associations and implied variance and covariance relationships with observed sample variances and covariances (See Bollen, 1989). A maximum likelihood fitting function is the basis for assessing goodness of fit. Maximum likelihood estimates are presented for the coefficients of the measurement model, which relates the survey items to latent variables, and the structural model, which relates latent variables to one another.

5. RESULTS

Sample size limitations preclude estimating the full model depicted in Figure 6.1 simultaneously. Consequently, the analysis proceeds in three steps. In the first step the relation between environmental variables and ABC project outcomes (OVERALL) is examined. Untabulated results indicate that the only environmental variables that exhibit significant direct associations with OVERALL are the reward environment (REWARD) of the site and the quality of existing information systems (INFOQUAL). Beliefs that individual performance is rewarded at the site (high reward expectancy) are positively associated with evaluations of the ABC system. Beliefs that existing information systems provide adequate, accurate information are negatively associated with evaluations of the ABC system, suggesting that ABC adds little in environments with good information systems.

In the second stage of analysis the relation between contextual variables and local management involvement (MINVOLVE) in the ABC project is examined. The only environmental variable that exhibits a significant relation with MINVOLVE is the reward environment; high reward expectancy is positively related to local management involvement in the ABC project.

In the final step, the model is estimated, retaining only those contextual variables that were associated with evaluations of the ABC system or local managers' involvement in the ABC project in earlier steps (INFOQUAL and REWARD).

One additional contextual variable, the quality of historical labor-management relations (LABOR), is introduced as a potential precursor of union support of the ABC project. Table 6.3 presents coefficient estimates of the structural equation model for the relation between ABC implementation process variables, the limited set of contextual variables and respondents' overall evaluation of the ABC system.

The results indicate that three process variables positively influence respondents' overall evaluation of the ABC system: top management and union support of the ABC project and the adequacy of resources devoted to the project. The significant associations of the reward environment and the quality of existing information systems on overall evaluations that were discovered in the first step of the analysis persist. However, when total effects are considered, the positive indirect effect of high quality information systems acting through local managers' involvement in the ABC project offsets the negative direct effect on the overall evaluation of the ABC system. Also, the relation between local management involvement and the reward environment (step 2, above) disappears when the direct influence of the reward environment on system evaluations is estimated simultaneously. Local management involvement is positively associated with top management support and with the quality of existing information systems. Union support of the ABC project is associated positively with local management support and with the quality of historical labor relations. The adequacy of resources devoted to the ABC project appears to be influenced more by top management support than by local management support of the ABC project. We might expect this result to differ between companies, since one company systematically assisted the sites in staffing ABC projects with consultants and corporate employees; however, as we will see in Chapter 7, the result holds for both companies.

The results provide face validity of the proposed description of the firms' ABC implementation process and the relationships between project management variables. Top management support is directly associated with local management awareness of and involvement in the ABC implementation project. Local management plays a gatekeeper role in assuring local union support and there is no evidence that top management intervenes in this relation. In contrast, local managers' knowledge of and involvement with the ABC project has little relation to whether the development team is provided adequate resources. Whether the project is believed to have an adequate resource endowment is related to top management support.

Table 6.3. Maximum Likelihood Estimation of the Relation Between Contextual and ABC Project Management Variables and Overall ABC Implementation Success

Maximum likelihood estimates of the coefficients of the structural model and t-statistics (in parentheses). The sample (N=112) includes only observations with no missing values. The results are qualitatively similar when data imputation methods are employed. Two measures of overall model fit are provided: Bentler's (1989) Comparative Fit Index (CFI) and the Root Mean Square Error of Approximation (RMSEA) with its 90 percent confidence interval. Bootstrapping methods (500 samples with replacement) are used to generate approximate p-values (two-tail) for the significance of the total effects of contextual and procedural variables on OVERALL. The p-values are approximations because bootstrapping methods do not make distributional assumptions.

	Estimated Direct Effects				Estimated Total Effects (approximate p-value)
	OVERALL	MINVOLVE	USUPPORT	RESOURCES	
Independent Variables					
MSUPPORT	.20 (1.68) *	.30 (4.02) ***	-.19 (1.63)	.17 (2.33) **	.29 (.012) **
MINVOLVE	-.35 (1.21)		.86 (3.08) ***	.21 (1.47)	.10 (.735)
USUPPORT	.34 (2.50) **				.34 (.016) **
RESOURCES	.76 (2.58) ***				.76 (.042) **
INFOQUAL	-.25 (2.08) **	.18 (1.92) *			-.23 (.132)
REWARD	.19 (1.96) **	.07 (.87)			.19 (.042) **
LABOR			.17 (2.00) **		.06 (.030) **
Model Fit Statistics	$R^2 = .56$	$R^2 = .55$	$R^2 = .39$	$R^2 = .44$	CFI=.932 RMSEA=.054, 90% C.I.= [.039, .068]

***, **, * Statistically significant at the p< 0.01, 0.05 or 0.10 (two-tail) level

Finding that top management support and adequate project resources are significantly related to evaluations of ABC systems replicates results of Shields (1995), Foster and Swenson (1997) and several case studies. The distinction between the importance of top management support (MSUPPORT) and the seeming irrelevance of local management support (MINVOLVE) is a new finding, as is the importance of employee-level involvement (USUPPORT). Foster and Swenson's (1997) survey respondents (job title unknown) report that line workers rarely use ABC data, and indeed, we find no evidence that the companies in our study disseminated ABC data to line workers. Thus, our finding of a significant association between ABC system evaluations and union support may reflect unique aspects of deploying ABC in a union setting.

6. SUMMARY

The research results of this chapter support the claim that evaluations of ABC systems are related to the process by which the organization develops and gains employee support for the systems. However, we also find that environmental factors that are outside of the scope of the ABC development project influence respondents' evaluation of project outcomes. Specifically, in environments in which individual performance is not linked to rewards and in settings in which existing information systems are believed to provide accurate, timely data, respondents are unlikely to evaluate ABC systems favorably. These environmental factors bear little relation to the process of implementing ABC; rather they affect evaluations of the ABC system directly. Thus, the process of instituting organizational change matters; however, there remain institutional settings in which ABC systems are unlikely to be valued.[6]

NOTES

[1] See Cooper & Turney (1990); Foster & Gupta (1990) and Cooper & Kaplan, (1991).

[2] By some estimates only 10% of all firms that adopt ABC continue to use it (Ness and Cucuzza, 1995).

[3] See Shield, (1995) and Foster & Swenson (1997).

[4] In the sections that follow, parenthetic words in BOLD font refer to specific variables. These variables are related to organizational theory in Table 6.1, are described in Table 6.2.

[5] The analysis treats as missing both items with no response and selection of the "Not Applicable" response. "Not Applicable" was offered selectively as an option for some questions related to ABC where we anticipated problems of inadequate knowledge and wanted to guard against forcing a "neutral" response of '3'.

Chapter 7

GOALS OF ABC IMPLEMENTATION AND MEANS OF ATTAINMENT

1. OVERVIEW

Chapter 6 investigated determinants of ABC implementation success using an overall measure of ABC system effectiveness. Previous studies employ similar composite evaluation scales; however, a limitation of this approach is that it does not permit exploration of multi-dimensional aspects of system effectiveness. One objective of this research is to provide evidence on the criteria that managers use in evaluating ABC systems and to investigate the claim that determinants of ABC project outcomes differ depending on which criteria are considered (e.g., Cooper *et al.*, 1992). Foster and Swenson (1997) describe three evaluation measures that researchers use as components of overall ABC system evaluation. Although the components have logical appeal, they are not predicated on formal scale development methods. The field-research approach of this study allows us to investigate the evaluation criteria used by survey respondents to assess ABC system effectiveness.

Content analysis of interviews conducted with 236 of the 265 survey respondents reveals two widely held views of what defines an effective ABC system: whether ABC data are used in product cost reduction or process improvement; and, whether ABC data are more accurate than data from the traditional cost system. We estimate a model of the likelihood of defining ABC system effectiveness as a function of perceived data accuracy and find that the respondent's job title is the only statistically significant determinant of whether this view is held. Respondents with production-related jobs are more likely to evaluate the ABC system based on perceived improvements in cost accuracy than are respondents in administrative roles, who place greater emphasis on whether ABC data are used in cost reduction. Differences in opinions are unrelated to company, competitive environment, whether the respondent is a system developer or whether the respondent reported receiving ABC training.

We also investigate whether different environmental conditions and ABC project management variables influence these components of overall ABC system effectiveness by repeating the analysis of Chapter 6, substituting survey data on accuracy and use of ABC data for overall evaluation of the ABC system. We find that ABC implementation is multi-dimensional, with different contextual and process variables influencing each component. Sensitivity analysis reveals additional company-specific and respondent group-specific determinants of perceived system accuracy and use; however, the findings of multi-dimensionality of overall system evaluations and differences in determinants of system use and accuracy are robust across respondent sub-samples. The results complement previous case studies and provide systematic evidence that implementing ABC with the objective of increasing cost system accuracy places different demands on the organization than does implementation aimed at generating data to support process improvement.

2. RESEARCH QUESTION

Foster and Swenson (1997) identify four measures of ABC project outcomes that have been widely used in the empirical management accounting literature: 1) overall success as judged by the evaluator, 2) use in decision making, 3) evidence of different decisions arising with use of ABC data; and, 4) improvements (in dollars) resulting from use of ABC data. Using survey data from a sample of 166 firms that use ABC, the authors document somewhat different correlates of success along each of these dimensions. The results suggest that firms use ABC systems to achieve different objectives and that attainment of different objectives depends on different factors. What is unknown is whether the measures developed by researchers are consistent with criteria embedded in managers' overall evaluations (e.g., whether the measures exhibit internal validity). We use field research methods to explore this question and to provide further evidence on determinants of different aspects of ABC system effectiveness. Specifically, we examine:

1. the criteria against which managers and ABC system developers evaluate ABC implementation success; and

2. whether the associations examined in the three previous research questions in Chapter 6 differ between component measures of the overall ABC system evaluation.

3. GOALS FOR ABC PROJECTS AS THE BASIS FOR EVALUATING PROJECT OUTCOMES

As in previous studies, in Chapter 6 we employed an overall evaluation of the ABC system (OVERALL) that allows respondents to self-define the evaluation criteria. However, as research question 1 above indicates, this raises the question: "What criteria do managers use in forming an overall assessment of ABC systems?" We conducted content analysis of 236 taped interviews to explore this question.[1] Full text transcripts of the 236 interviews were searched for key words related to ABC system evaluations. Search results yielded 129 respondents' opinions.[2] The 129 respondents represent 20 of the 21 sites and are split in approximately the same proportion as the survey respondents between the firms and between ABC developers and managers. After identifying discussions of ABC system evaluation, the transcripts were read independently by a researcher and a research assistant. Three evaluation criteria emerged: 1) use of ABC data for cost reduction; 2) use of ABC data for process improvements; and, 3) improved accuracy of product cost information relative to the traditional cost system. The researcher and research assistant independently coded the responses as belonging primarily to one of the three categories. Although respondents occasionally combined the first and second criteria in their discussion, very few respondents discussed the third criterion in conjunction with either of the others. Consequently, we combine the first and second groups to form two groups who differ in the way that they define an effective ABC system. In the first group, 67 respondents define effectiveness as use of ABC data in cost reduction or process improvements. In the second group, 47 respondents believe that increased cost accuracy defines an effective ABC system.[3]

We used contingency tables to evaluate the association between opinions about evaluation criteria and: the respondents' company; whether the respondent worked in a plant that faced significant external competition; whether the respondent was an ABC system developer; whether the respondent claimed to have received training in ABC; and the respondent's job title. Comparing differences between respondents who evaluated ABC system effectiveness based on use in cost reduction or process improvement with those who base their opinion on improved accuracy of cost data, respondents' job title is the only significant determinant of which view is held.[4] The same result is obtained in a multivariate analysis. Respondents with jobs that are linked to production (e.g., engineering, materials management, production operations, quality control) are significantly more likely to evaluate the ABC system based on whether it provides more accurate costs than are respondents in administrative roles (e.g., plant manager, finance and accounting, information systems, human resource management). The latter group places greater emphasis on whether ABC data are used in cost reduction or process improvement. Differences in opinions are unrelated to the respondent's firm, whether the respondent works in a site that faces significant competition, whether the respondent is a system developer or whether the respondent received ABC training.

The results of the content analysis are consistent with case study evidence from Cooper et al. (1992) that firms typically adopt ABC with one of two objectives: increased product cost accuracy (e.g., for inventory valuation and cost-based decisions) or use in process improvement (e.g.," activity based management"). Cooper *et al.* (1992) hypothesize that different implementation processes are required as a function of ABC project objectives. Foster and Swenson (1997) provide preliminary evidence that different evaluation measures are correlated with different implementation process variables. We explore this issue, posed in research question 2, by substituting for the OVERALL measure of success in Figure 6.1, measures of ABC data accuracy (ACCURACY) and ABC system use (USE) developed from the survey data.

3.1 Determinants of ABC System Use and Perceived Accuracy

Following the same three stage approach that we used in Chapter 6 to combat data limitations, we first estimate the relation between environmental conditions and ABC project outcomes--- substituting ACCURACY and USE for OVERALL (results untabulated). Compared with the overall evaluation of the ABC system, a larger set of contextual variables is associated with respondents' beliefs about the use and accuracy of ABC data and many of the new explanatory variables are individual rather than organizational environmental factors. Environmental variables associated with at least one of the measures are: the reward environment (REWARD), the quality of existing information systems (INFOQUAL), commitment of the respondent to the organization (COMMIT), the respondent's attitude toward change (CHANGE), the perceived importance of the site (IMPPLT), and the likelihood of employee layoffs at the site (LAYOFF).

Table 7.1 repeats the analysis of Table 6.3, substituting ACCURACY and USE for OVERALL and including all contextual variables found to directly influence either variable. The results support the proposition that different factors influence different criterion for evaluating ABC systems. The only process variable that influences ACCURACY is adequacy of resources devoted to the ABC project (RESOURCES). Notably absent are significant direct or indirect effects of top managers, local managers or the union. This result suggests a mechanical relation, like a production function, linking project inputs to the quality of data outputs. The only environmental condition variable associated with perceived data accuracy is the respondent's felt need for change in local work practices (CHANGE). The more that an individual agrees that changes are needed the more likely they are to ascribe increased accuracy to ABC data. Notably absent is a significant relation between the quality of existing information systems and accuracy of ABC data. Combined with the results of Table 6.3 this suggests that while high quality information systems may substitute for ABC systems in meeting managers' information needs, they are not necessarily complementary in the sense of providing better data from which to design ABC systems that generate more accurate data.

Table 7.1. Maximum likelihood estimation of determinants of and two aspects of ABC implementation success
Maximum likelihood estimates of the coefficients of the structural model and t-statistics (in parentheses).

Independent Variables	Estimated Direct Effects					Estimated Total Effects (approximate p-values)	
	ACCURACY	USE	MINVOLVE	USUPPORT	RESOURCES	ACCURACY	USE
MSUPPORT	-.07 (.69)	.14 (1.76)*	.34 (4.91)***	.04 (.41)	.23 (3.19)***	.18 (.125)	.32 (.009)***
MINVOLVE	.04 (.21)	.06 (.49)		.68 (3.40)***	.08 (.69)	.15 (.399)	.22 (.315)
USUPPORT	.06 (.78)	.19 (3.07)***				.06 (.409)	.19 (.033)**
RESOURCES	.85 (4.08)***	.40 (3.08)***				.85 (.008)***	.40 (.028)**
INFOQUAL	-.04	.03 (.31)	.16 (1.90)*			.02 (.294)	.06 (.595)
COMMIT	.03 (.17)	-.30 (2.31)**				.03 (.977)	-.30 (.076)*
CHANGE	.47 (2.97)***	.25 (2.22)**				.47 (.034)**	.25 (.156)
IMPPLT	-.05 (.60)	.04 (.69)				-.05 (.604)	.04 (.586)
LAYOFF	.00 (.06)	-.09 (1.87)*				.00 (.845)	-.10 (.092)*
REWARD	.00 (.00)	.25 (3.27)***	.11 (1.66)*			.02 (.861)	.27 (.015)**
LABOR				.16 (1.78)*		.01 (.286)	.03 (.061)*
Model Fit Statistics	$R^2 = .50$	$R^2 = .84$	$R^2 = .50$	$R^2 = .31$	$R^2 = .31$	CFI=.900 RMSEA=.044, 90% C.I. = [.037, .050]	

***, **, * Statistically significant at the p< 0.01, 0.05 or 0.10 (two-tail) level

In contrast to ACCURACY, USE of ABC data is related to top management and union support of the ABC project and adequacy of resources devoted to the project. Consistent with the results of Table 6.3, local management involvement in the ABC project appears to play no role in whether data from the ABC system are used at the site. Compared to ACCURACY, the attainment of which is mechanistically related to project inputs, USE of ABC data depends on both social and technical factors. Contextual variables that influence USE include the respondent's commitment to the organization and felt need for change in the organization, the likelihood of employee layoffs and the reward environment. Together these variables suggest that use of ABC data imposes a large personal cost on employees. Employees will sustain these costs if they are committed to the organization, if they believe that the organization is committed to them (low layoff prospects) and is prepared to reward individual performance, and if they believe that there are opportunities for enacting changes that will improve performance at the site.

3.2 Company, Site and Respondent Effects on the Determinants of ABC Project Outcomes

A concern in pooling responses from two companies and two respondent groups (managers and ABC system developers) is that separate models may be warranted for a particular sub-group. For that matter, because our sites were selected to represent the full range of ABC implementation experience of each firm, some sites have greater experience with the ABC model than others. Consequently, it is reasonable to wonder whether more mature sites feel similarly about the determinants of system effectiveness as newer implementation sites. We investigated the stability of our results across three subdivisions of the data: 1) firms, 2) managers versus ABC system developers, and 3) mature versus more recent ABC implementations.

We find that discriminating between firms or between managers and ABC system developers does not yield significantly different models. Although the magnitude of the effect of a particular variable in the model may be more for one group than the other, the variables that are significant are the same. In contrast, we find marked differences in the way that respondents from mature sites view ABC system effectiveness as compared to respondents from relatively new ABC implementations. Specifically, while the model of product cost ACCURACY is stable across both groups, the model of ABC system USE is quite different between early and late adopters.

The stability of our results over companies and respondent populations is comforting because it gives us greater confidence that we are observing broad behavioral patterns that could be expected to hold in a different set of firms.

The variation within firms between early and late adopters of ABC is also somewhat comforting in that it was diversity in the experience implementing ABC that prompted the firms to allow us to conduct our research. Nonetheless we must be a bit cautious in interpreting the differences between early and late adopters as indicative of a general maturation process of an organizational change. The maturity of the model may reflect several things. As we discussed in Chapter 2, the ABC implementation literature has been characterized as proceeding in stages with different factors affecting successful transition between stages. Consequently, instability in determinants of ABC system accuracy or use could reflect sites at different stages of implementation. Alternatively, with greater experience with ABC, respondents from more mature sites may be better informed and thus could represent the "true" model, while respondents from newer sites could be articulating their expectations relative to uncertain future uses ABC data. Finally, we must remember that sites are not randomly selected for ABC implementation. Differences between early and adopters could reflect systematic differences in the environment that we have not adequately measured but which caused certain sites to be more or less amenable to ABC than others. In the remaining discussion we highlight some key differences in the submodel investigations.

Considering first the comparisons of firms and of respondents, we first mention results from the original model that are unaffected by dividing the sample in these ways. Factors affecting USE or ACCURACY which remain significant for both sub-sample models include positive relations between:

- perceived ABC data accuracy and respondents' attitude toward change;
- use of ABC data and union support of the ABC project; and,
- use of ABC data and the perceived reward environment at the site.

Although, overall, the models were not determined to be significantly different between firms or between respondents, individual differences did emerge. Relationships that were identified as significant in the pooled sample, but which appear to be company-specific include relations between:[5]

- use of ABC data and top management support, which is confined to company 1; and,
- use of ABC data and adequacy of project resources, respondents' attitude toward change, and the probability of employee layoffs, which are confined to company 2.

Relationships that were identified as significant in the full sample, but which appear to be respondent type-specific include relations between:

- accuracy of ABC data and adequacy of resources provided to the ABC project, which is confined to managers; and,
- use of ABC data and adequacy of project resources and the probability of employee layoffs, which are confined to ABC system developers.

In the first case, it is likely that ABC project developers have an incentive to uniformly claim inadequacy of resources since data accuracy may be viewed as reflecting the quality of ABC system development work. Similarly, managers, who are typically responsible for using ABC data, have an incentive to attribute their failure to use the data to inadequacies in the project development. In short, in appears that opinions about resource adequacy for the project may be shaped by respondents' incentives to shift blame for failure to obtain more accurate data from the ABC system or failure to use ABC data after the system is developed.

Turning now to the comparison of sites that adopted ABC relatively early within a firm as compared to those that adopted relatively late, we find rather marked differences. Table 7.2 reports the original model[6] with pooled data as well as the models estimated for mature and for more recent ABC implementation sites. The major differences are in the portion of the model that relates contextual and process factors to USE of the ABC data for cost reduction. The portions of the model related to ACCURACY are remarkably stable, as are the portions of the model that relate contextual factors to the process of ABC implementation (lower half of Table 7.2).

Stability in the determinants of ACCURACY suggest that assessment of accuracy is a natural artifact of installing *any* ABC system and neither subsequent revisions to the system nor a respondent's re-evaluation of accuracy dramatically change the underlying model. In short, the model of ACCURACY is "durable" --- unaffected by different stages of implementation, by firms' priority for implementing at the site or by changes in respondents' information about costs or benefits of implementation. Similarly, the relation between contextual factors and the process of ABC implementation appears to be quite stable. The reward environment appears to have played a more important role in local management involvement during early ABC implementations, while the quality of existing information systems played a more important role in local management involvement in later ABC implementations. This seems to suggest differences between the types of plants that were chosen or that volunteered to implement ABC early rather than late; however, as noted earlier we cannot unambiguously rule out other explanations.

Table 7.2. **Stability Of The Relation Between Contextual And Process Variables And Two Components Of Overall ABC Implementation Success: Effects Of ABC System Maturity**

Maximum likelihood estimates of the coefficients (*t*-statistics in parentheses) of the direct effects of contextual and process variables on ABC system accuracy and use. To permit the estimation of two sub-models, summated scales replace the latent variables used in earlier analyses. The first model repeats the analysis of Chapter 7 using summated scales. Model 2 examines the durability of relations estimated in the model by segmenting the data into two roughly equal sized groups based on the date when the first ABC model was completed. Ten sites where ABC was implemented prior to May 1993 are termed "mature" implementations, while those that completed ABC implementation during the latter part of 1993 and 1994 are termed "recent" implementations relative to the data collection period.

Dependent Variable (Summated Scale)	Independent Variables	Model 1: Full Sample (N=199)		Model 2: Split by Model Maturity			
				Mature Models N=97		Recent Models N=102	
ACCURACY			$R^2=.19$		$R^2=.21$		$R^2=.23$
	MSUPPORT	.02 (.32)		.02 (.22)		.01 (.07)	
	MINVOLVE	.05 (.84)		.06 (.79)		.03 (.35)	
	USUPPORT	.01 (.10)		.11 (1.12)		-.13 (1.21)	
	RESOURCES	.35 (4.55) ***		.34 (3.21) ***		.35 (3.13) ***	
	INFOQUAL	-.01 (.15)		-.03 (0.39)		-.03 (.40)	
	COMMIT	.04 (.78)		.10 (1.13)		.04 (.57)	
	CHANGE	.22 (2.92) ***		.23 (2.22) **		.26 (2.44) **	
	IMPPLT	-.01 (.16)		-.14 (1.53)		.05 (.66)	
	LAYOFF	-.03 (.44)		-.01 (.04)		-.09 (1.04)	
	REWARD	.02 (.35)		-.00 (.04)		.04 (.51)	
USE			$R^2=.46$		$R^2=.56$		$R^2=.45$
	MSUPPORT	.24 (3.25) ***		.35 (3.87) ***		.11 (.93)	
	MINVOLVE	.12 (1.82) *		.13 (1.39)		.08 (.86)	
	USUPPORT	.30 (3.27) ***		.29 (2.53) **		.35 (2.52) **	
	RESOURCES	.11 (1.96) **		.02 (.16)		.46 (3.29) ***	
	INFOQUAL	.00 (.01)		-.07 (.86)		.16 (1.63)	
	COMMIT	-.10 (1.57)		-.09 (.94)		-.12 (1.42)	
	CHANGE	.20 (2.17) **		.17 (1.47)		.14 (1.98) **	
	IMPPLT	.05 (.68)		.15 (1.40)		-.05 (.54)	
	LAYOFF	-.23 (2.75) ***		-.22 (1.47)		-.28 (2.54) ***	
	REWARD	.23 (4.21) ***		.25 (3.57) ***		.14 (1.67) *	
MINVOLVE			$R^2=.32$		$R^2=.21$		$R^2=.42$
	MSUPPORT	.47 (6.57) ***		.31 (3.14) ***		.64 (6.39) ***	
	REWARD	.14 (2.41) **		.16 (2.02) **		.09 (0.98)	
	INFOQUAL	.17 (2.49) **		.07 (.75)		.30 (2.90) ***	
USUPPORT			$R^2=.22$		$R^2=.26$		$R^2=.17$
	LABOR	.09 (1.95) *		.08 (.98)		.09 (1.27)	
	MINVOLVE	.23 (4.91) ***		.32 (4.54) ***		.14 (2.24) ***	
	MSUPPORT	.08 (1.53)		.06 (0.80)		.11 (1.53)	
RESOURCES			$R^2=.18$		$R^2=.11$		$R^2=.27$
	MSUPPORT	.23 (4.80) ***		.20 (3.01) ***		.28 (3.88) ***	
	MINVOLVE	.06 (1.42)		.02 (0.24)		.09 (1.55)	
Model Fit Statistics	CFI	.951		.922			
	RMSEA, 90% C.I.	.074, [.044, .100]		.068, [.045, .090]			

***, **, * Statistically significant at the *p*< 0.01, 0.05 or 0.10 (two-tail) level

Turning to determinants of USE, the model differs substantially between mature and recent implementation sites. Since USE is something that emerges (or doesn't) over time after completion of the ABC system, it is reasonable that this measure of ABC implementation effectiveness is vulnerable to model instability over time. For sites with mature implementations, respondents' assessment of USE is related significantly to top management support, union support and the reward environment. For sites with more recent implementations, USE is also related to union support and to the reward environment; however, it is not related to top management support and the reward environment has a smaller influence than for mature sites. In addition to these factors, adequacy of resources, respondents' commitment to change, and the likelihood of layoffs are determinants of USE in this setting. Differences in the role of top management are consistent with top management taking pains to promote the ABC program early in its existence but becoming less visible as implementation proceeds. These differences are also consistent with mature sites experiencing pressure to use the data that sites with more recent implementations have not yet experienced --- a shift in top managers' expectations that occurs with model maturity. The former explanation points to real differences in the implementation experience of early versus late adopters while the latter explanation points to differences that stem from the stage of implementation of the site. The data do not permit us to distinguish between these explanations.

Among the other determinants of USE that differ between the two sub-samples, only the effect of RESOURCES is quite different in magnitude and significance. (Commitment to change and the likelihood of layoffs are marginally significant even for the mature sites and the magnitude of the coefficients is similar.) Since RESOURCES refers to the project resources associated with ABC system development, this result seems to suggest that mature sites no longer depend on the ABC development team (or maintenance team) to drive the use of the ABC data. This interpretation is consistent with the hypothesis advanced by Cooper *et al*. (1992), that moving from "implementation to action" requires a different group of people to become involved in using ABC data than was involved in creating the data. They state:

> A more fundamental cause of the delays in taking action may have been inadequate preparation of the organization for changes in thinking and decision making...The most successful projects occurred when a specific target for change was identified early in the project ... The target was the person or group whose decisions were expected to change as a consequence of the information. (p. 8)

That recent implementations rely heavily on ABC developers to promote use of the data hints at a transition period during which those who are familiar with the system help users to identify problems to which the system lends itself.

In summary, stability of the model of determinants of ABC system effectiveness over time depends upon the measure of effectiveness that one considers. The relations between contextual and process factors and between these factors and ACCURACY are quite stable. The relation between these factors and USE is not stable. We cannot unambiguously distinguish between explanations related to real differences in the implementations of early versus late adopters, differences in the implementation stages that early and late adopters are in at the time of our data collection, and differences in the knowledge that respondents have about ABC implementation and its subsequent outcomes. All of these explanations are plausible and have distinct implications for managing ABC implementation. Consequently, future research aimed at disentangling these factors is needed.

4. SUMMARY

This chapter provides the first systematic evidence that, when asked to evaluate ABC systems, respondents' use different criterion. Content analysis of interview transcripts reveals two widely held views: that ABC systems are valuable if they provide more accurate cost data than the traditional cost system; or if there is evidence that ABC data are used for cost reduction or process improvement. The respondent's job title is the only significant factor in explaining differences in opinions. Respondents with jobs that are closely linked to production operations are more likely to evaluate the ABC system against a criterion of data accuracy, while respondents in support functions are more likely to require evidence of use in cost reduction.

Consistent with preliminary evidence from case studies, we find that good performance along different criteria is associated with different environmental and ABC project management factors. The perceived accuracy of ABC data is influenced by adequacy of resources devoted to ABC system development and by the attitude of the respondent toward the need for change at the site. In contrast, use of ABC data is influenced by several project management variables including: top management support and union support of the ABC project, and adequacy of project resources. Contextual variables that influence respondents' assessment of the degree to which ABC data are used include: the respondent's commitment to the organization and belief that change in management practices is needed, the likelihood of employee layoffs, and the degree to which individual performance is rewarded. In summary, achieving increased cost accuracy appears to depend on a relationship that resembles a production function, in that the accuracy of data outputs is related to the quality of project inputs. In contrast, use of ABC data depends critically upon a wider array of contextual and process factors. Differences in the determinants of these criteria for evaluating ABC systems adds meaning to the advice frequently offered to ABC developers: to design systems that meet managerial decision-making needs. It also implies that, perhaps more than specifications of the ABC model, the implementation process itself should differ as a function of whether the chief objective is providing more accurate costs or providing fundamentally different types of cost data that will be useful in process improvement or cost reduction.

---

[1] An analysis software package designed for non-numerical, unstructured data (NU.DIST®) was used. The researcher codes interview passages related to constructs of interest and attributes of the interviewee. The software uses these codes to create a structured index that is useful for investigating systematic response patterns.

[2] Some interviewees did not believe that they had sufficient knowledge about ABC systems to offer an opinion about what system effectiveness, while others were not asked to discuss the issue.

[3] Ten respondents (7.8%) offered opinions that were sufficiently unusual that they were discarded. Five respondents offered valid but very different responses and thus are not included in subsequent analysis.

[4] Observed differences in opinions between managers of different functions, in conjunction with theoretical support for these differences in the organizational literature, is further evidence that previous studies, which focus on the opinions of accounting professionals, contain potentially biased results.

[5] Although our knowledge of the companies suggests why some of these relations might exist, we are not at liberty to share these casual explanations because they would identify the companies to a reader with industry knowledge.

[6] The results differ somewhat from those reported in Chapter 7 because summated scales were used to represent each variable for the much smaller sample sizes of the sub models. The pooled results are repeated using these scales for comparability.

Chapter 8

WHAT HAVE WE LEARNED?

This study has been designed to address a number of issues regarding the implementation of activity based costing in two large, complex companies. As discussed in Chapter 4, General Motors and Chrysler's adoption and deployment of ABC, was the result of a felt need for change; however, both organizations experienced many twists and turns as they wrestled with the issues of implementation. The experiences of these firms document our central contention that ABC implementation *demands* significant organizational change. The influential factors in effecting organizational changes associated with ABC implementation are similar to those that have been widely documented in hundreds of studies of other organizational changes. We hope that our study provides an indication of the extent of change necessary.

The development of an ABC model requires the merging of detailed organization-specific knowledge and knowledge of the theoretical and conceptual model of activity based costing. As a result, large companies typically adopt a sequential, or in some cases multi-generation, strategy of implementing ABC at disparate sites using a team of local experts who have access to (and may be joined by) ABC specialists. A sequential strategy is typically dictated by scarcity and costs of ABC specialists and the capability of the firm to support parallel projects. One challenge of managing the sequential rollout of ABC is that at any given point in time different sites have different levels of experience with and expertise in using ABC data and as a result place different demands for support on the central administration. One firm in our study eventually separated implementation support from maintenance support in recognition of these differences. Another challenge is that the objectives for ABC may shift in the course of the rollout as the firm gains expertise with ABC and discovers new applications for the data. We find that determinants of "successful" implementation of ABC depend critically on the objectives of the project. Thus, to the extent that firm objectives for ABC change over time, the implementation process must be continually evaluated to insure the alignment of project resources with organizational objectives for each generation of new implementation projects.

This study contributes empirical evidence that evaluations of ABC systems are associated with organizational context and with the process of implementing ABC; and, that the association depends upon the evaluation measure under consideration. Four methodological differences distinguish this research from prior studies. First, most studies use the firm as the unit of analysis for studying determinants of successful ABC implementation. This approach ignores the fact that large firms typically develop many ABC models and that the organizational change literature has established that a necessary though insufficient condition for organizational change is changing the beliefs and behaviors of individuals affected by change. We address this limitation by using an embedded, multiple case study research design to study 21 ABC projects in two firms. A second limitation of previous studies is using attitudinal data gathered from accounting professionals and 'champions' of the ABC project. Aside from biases caused by self-interested informants and omission of the opinions of managers who are intended to use ABC data, organizational theory hypothesizes that functional perspectives shape individuals' opinions. Absent a self-reporting bias or systematic differences between ABC developers and users, these studies are likely to miss critical variation caused by different interpretations of the same event by managers in different functions. We address this limitation by including as critical informants all functional managers and ABC developers from a site. Prior studies of ABC projects have used mail surveys to analyze ABC projects from many firms or have provided descriptive evidence from case studies of individual ABC projects. We provide a complementary perspective by combining standardized data collection methods (surveys) with systematic field-based research. Finally, previous studies have employed measures of success defined *ex ante* by the researcher. This study uses an overall measure of ABC system effectiveness and two constituent measures that are defined by study participants. Allowing respondents to define criteria for evaluating ABC systems in responses to open-ended questions increases the likelihood that measures purported to represent the components of overall evaluations explain a large portion of observed variance in overall evaluations.

These research design choices distinguish this study and define its contribution to the literature; however, as with all exploratory studies important limitations remain. First, the study is conducted in two firms from a single industry. We provide evidence on the robustness of our results across company and respondent-type sub-groups; nonetheless, the empirical results may not generalize to other firms, other industry settings or other informants. Second, the data reflect opinions and attitudes of respondents who are assumed to be informed and truthful. Although we identify respondents who we believe are informed and we use survey design and analysis methods aimed at reducing the likelihood of "random" responses and mitigating measurement error, we remain vulnerable to systematic response bias. Moreover, the attitudinal data are not calibrated against objective data sources. This limitation reflects widespread disagreement among researchers about how to unambiguously measure performance of cost systems as well as the fact that many of the variables are fundamentally latent (unobserved).

In a close look at team effectiveness, we studied the relation of team dynamics and composition to the time to develop ABC models and the complexity of the model. We examined the implementation process of 18 plants of two major automobile manufacturers in the U.S. from the perspective of ABC development teams. The contribution here is twofold. The size and overall composition of the teams were comparable at both firms, but differed significantly within firms, with more manufacturing personnel being represented on Company B's teams. Team size and the level of resources to perform the task were issues of concern for many team members. The ABC models developed by the team were characterized by looking at three variables. Company A used fewer activity centers and had fewer 1st and 2nd stage cost drivers for both Core and Non Core plants. As mentioned earlier, this is difficult to interpret given the complexities involved at each site. In addition, in almost all cases (except for 1st stage drivers), the number of activity centers and 1st and 2nd stage cost drivers were greater for *Non Core* teams than for *Core* teams, but not to any significant degree.

Our results also indicate that understanding the linkages among a several variables is important in order to reduce development time. As a starting point, ABC teams must be well educated. Education not only involves careful attention to fundamental concepts but also entails seeing the ties among well-designed manufacturing (or service) operations, well-specified ABC models and overall cost competitiveness. Education, then, must go beyond cost management methods and focus on firm strategy and growth. It also appears that ABC training cannot rest solely with ABC team members or managers, but must be pushed down to the lowest levels of each firm so that those at the point of manufacturing (or service) understand how their actions ultimately influenced costs and performance.

Second, the impact of external competition is another significant factor that must be considered. While we were in the field, we experienced strike activity due to outsourcing first hand at several of the components' plants. Thus, outside competition is a very real threat to *Non Core* plants in the automobile industry, and it is becoming much more of a concern to *Core* plants whose technology and products are being threatened by both domestic and foreign competition. It could be the case that companies who have not been successful with ABC did not feel the urgency as some of these plants did to implement an ABC model. This may be the case especially in companies that may not be competing on cost as their primary strategy.

How teams perceive the significance of their task will be affected by both of these factors. Fostering team cohesiveness is another critical finding of this part of our study. Being able to resolve conflicts and understanding how significant the task is will have strong effects on the level of team cohesion. In turn, as teams become more cohesive the time to develop ABC models will decrease.

On average, it took the sites in our study 7 months to develop an initial ABC model; however this average conceals differences in staffing and model complexity that influenced time to project completion. Left to staff an ABC project with local resources in a climate of constrained headcount, local managers typically did not comply with the recommendation to use a dedicated, multi-disciplinary team. This might cause some to argue that we have not studied "best practice" in ABC implementation. We believe, however, that our sites are representative of outcomes that are likely when the benefits of ABC implementation accrue primarily to the firm while the costs of ABC implementation reside primarily at local sites. The managerial implication of this is that the firm may need to subsidize initial implementation to achieve the desired results or a stronger case for the benefits of ABC data for local managers must be made.

A final implication of our study is that management innovations such as ABC have very close ties to other innovations such as total quality management, business process reengineering and performance scorecards. The differences among these innovations are what each innovation emphasizes (e.g., improving quality of process or products versus controlling or reducing costs of processes or products or developing an integrated performance measurement system). Since many innovations involve major organizational change, management can infer that if their organization succeeds with one type of innovation, then there is a good chance of success for the next kind of innovation. Thus, the lessons learned in our study on ABC can be applied with the appropriate adjustments to just about any management innovation since many require major organizational change.

Chapter 9

WHERE ARE THEY NOW? REFLECTIONS ON THE PAST FIVE YEARS

1. OVERVIEW

The genesis of ABC at General Motors Corporation and at what is now the Chrysler Group of Daimler-Chrysler AG can be traced to the mid and late 1980's, respectively. As researchers, we were privileged to observe and interact with these firms throughout the 1990's, when ABC was rolled out to all manufacturing locations and some administrative functions. Our most intensive interactions occurred in 1995, with extensive visits to 21 ABC implementation sites and interviews with 265 managers and ABC team members. Using these data and historical archives from the ABC systems, the preceding chapters provide a piercing look at the first decade of ABC through the lens of two large companies that chose to adopt and implement it. However, we would be remiss if we did not consider how events of recent years --- including dramatic changes in the boundaries and ownership of both firms, advances in information technology, and a booming U.S. consumer market --- have affected the ABC initiative. In this chapter we provide an update on the ABC initiatives. With the help of experienced corporate managers who have been involved for many years with ABC, we reflect on what ABC was, what it is today, what is envisioned for the future.

2. GENERAL MOTORS CORPORATION: THE FORM AND SUBSTANCE OF ABC IN 2001

Ironically, while ABC was intended to create a common approach to product costing from the patchwork of incompatible legacy systems from General Motors' early history of mergers and acquisitions, today ABC is itself a patchwork of initiatives. Within highly competitive areas of the firm, such as the Service Parts Organization (GM-SPO), and the non-core plants of our study (many of which were "privatized" with the formation of Delphi Automotive in 1998), ABC continues and has attained a high level of sophistication. For example, at GM-SPO, the integration of ABC with a new Enterprise Resource Planning (ERP) system, allows managers to evaluate costs by product, customer, and channel of distribution, and to perform dynamic "what-if" analysis and forecasting. The ABC model is refreshed as frequently as monthly and thus reflects current operational efficiencies and input costs. Moreover, like traditional variance analysis, it is now possible to analyze time trends for various aspects of operational and cost performance. In the early days of ABC it was possible with considerable effort to "slice" costs in a number of predefined ways; however, ABC-based forecasting required complex manipulation of cost system outputs, most of which was done "offline". Most ABC models were refreshed annually, at best, and many of these updates employed simplifying assumptions (e.g., employing an historical measure of the cost per unit cost driver rather than calculating it using data on both actual cost driver usage, actual capacity utilization and actual costs).

In more traditional, or "core" operations, such as metal stamping and powertrain operations, the development of ABC has, to varying degrees, stalled. Recall that ABC emerged in the stamping plants and that much of the early adaptation aimed at standardizing the approach for widespread rollout was pioneered in these facilities. Today ABC data continue to be used at the corporate level as a basis for comparing production costs among stamping plants. ABC data have never attained widespread use by plant-level managers as a basis for performance evaluation or for directing operational improvements. Of course this begs the question --- how do central managers obtain the detailed local data of ABC systems if local ABC development teams have been disbanded and ABC systems are not maintained? The answer reflects a hybrid, short-term approach to ABC and traditional labor-based cost systems. Specifically, the product cost data from previous ABC systems are translated to a labor-based burden rate, which are used to create current product costs. Variances to the new standard are written off on a current basis. Of course this approach will yield increasingly obsolete product costs as the reality of operations and business processes shift away from the activities and efficiencies that were reflected in the old ABC model. There are no plans at present to require plants to revisit these models.

In the powertrain plants, where ABC models were not overtly standardized and where corporate oversight and use of the data was not coordinated, we find quite different circumstances. In some plants ABC has been completely abandoned. In others, where the ABC models were developed to address local managers' problems, they continue to be maintained and used under the direction and support of local managers. Even in these latter cases however, there have been no major investments in new ABC software --- so the remaining "system" looks quite different from the very sophisticated management information system that we see at GM-SPO and quite rudimentary when compared to current software standards.

In sum, the heterogeneity in ABC implementation outcomes that motivated our detailed look at ABC projects in 1995 continues to persist at General Motors. ABC is neither a standardized routine nor an abandoned and forgotten "program of the month" --- it is all of these things, and the particular manifestation appears to be intimately related to the environment, the process by which ABC was implemented, and the people involved in its implementation. In subsequent sections we describe in greater detail how some of these factors have influenced ABC implementation since our 1995 data collection efforts.

3. CHRYSLER GROUP OF DAIMLER-CHRYSLER AG: THE FORM AND SUBSTANCE OF ABC IN 2001

Today Daimler-Chrysler is in the midst of the "third re-engineering of ABC" --- a part of a larger organizational initiation to design internally an integrated cost management system.

An internal memo that charts the evolution of ABC describes the years 1991-5 as the years of "plant specific" ABC models. One manager characterized the period as one in which "we really wanted to tailor our focus to plant needs --- what do you as a plant manager need to get from your cost management system that you don't today?" While this approach was tempered by the involvement of consultants and corporate ABC experts, who urged the use of certain "recommended" cost drivers and selection from a list of approximately 190 standard activities, the resulting models were nonetheless highly unique. A current senior finance manager recalls, "Data coming out of those models were so different. The methodology was so different between two stamping plants that when I tried to compare the activities on a certain kind of press between two plants I couldn't relate the numbers." Many times the problem was data availability --- "The drivers being suggested were the same, but the data available to quantify those drivers may have existed at one plant but not another. So the one plant would develop a 'pseudo-driver' and that ended up distorting plant-to-plant comparisons." Another problem was defining business processes..."We didn't do a very good job of trying to standardize the processes --- not only the activities, but the processes within the plants. We focused on getting better (but not very consistent) product costs and missed the boat on performance management."

A re-engineering of ABC that focused on limiting the cost drivers and business activities to a much smaller standardized set took place during 1994-8 and is termed the era of "standardized ABC." Standardization required developing software modules that served as "front end" preprocessing steps to ABC. One manager recalls,

> We built a data warehouse of output coming out of the ABC models to try to spread the data throughout the organization so that you could query on part number or another basis and see activities underneath the product. [The re-engineering] helped us make some headway on data comparability, but there were still major problems. The first problem was timing ...after implementation was done the maintenance process was still taking two to four months... the operating customer said, 'I've made thousands of decisions between the time you studied and today, so what you're giving me is so old that I can't use it.' Another challenge is that the model builders --- plant analysts --- were saying, 'OK, I understand that ABC gives me better part costs, but the plant managers and I aren't measured on part cost. We are measured on manufacturing efficiency. We are measured on the ability to attain and achieve cost reduction targets and I do that by managing functions not processes.' So for example, ABC was telling them the cost of running production line 123 but line 123 doesn't have a functional owner. There is a maintenance function that serves line 123, a material function that serves line 123 and a production group that serves line 123, but there is no group that manages the full line for total improved cost. So the data coming out of ABC was not helping managers do their job. We had this great process tool, but we don't have process managers so the data were old by the time they were available and they were not organized along familiar lines.

Interestingly, while most ABC models in the early 1990's were updated annually, Chrysler was updating their ABC data three times per year --- first a prospective "budget model" was developed, and then a mid-year and year-end "actual" model was built. In spite of this seemingly advanced state of information timeliness, managers continued to find ABC data obsolete on arrival.

At the end of 1996, overwhelmed with evidence that ABC was having a limited impact on operating managers' decisions and was creating a severe drain on plant-level resources, the mid-year and end of year updates were cancelled. The idea was to devote more resources to better planning and budget models, recognizing that ABC was serving a very limited use as a mechanism for performance evaluation. Of course this left unanswered the question of how to assign product costs. A manager describes the dilemma:

> ...one alternative was to go back to the traditional burden process that we got rid of ...we ended up with a modified process --- a hybrid between the ABC process ... and what we had done for 30 years, the burden rate process...The old process was departmental-based. The process that we

installed in 1997 was more process based, but we didn't get real fancy on cost drivers. So we might have reduced the number of first stage cost drivers for assigning costs from processes from eight to three and then our second stage process of assigning costs to products we threw out the window. We didn't do anything. We said that if widget A and B go through the same processes they consume overhead at the same rate --- not too different from the old burden rate process. This took us from an update taking more than six weeks to on average three or four business days. We said, 'we don't have good dollars to begin with, so let's not pretend that we do. Let's simplify the process. Let's get a little better at process costing, but if a part runs through the same process then so be it. There is no need for the second stage stuff. That's where we are now --- but it is a stopgap until the new cost management system is in place [at the end of 2000]. It's not where we want to be as far as having better part costs, but it's not as painful as it used to be.

The new cost management system, which was launched in August 1999 and is due to be complete in North America in December 2000, is intended to address several deficiencies in the ABC approach. And reminiscent of the challenges of replacing the traditional labor-burden system with ABC, its introduction has raised certain organizational challenges. The manager of the group charged with developing and introducing it described the process:

The first thing we did to replace ABC was not to call it ABC anymore because there was too much "baggage" within the company that we needed to leave behind. So we called it 'process costing.' ...We really made an effort to get it into the normal finance process. In the first and second iteration of ABC, it was always a secondary process --- never part of mainstream finance... We called it 'Monthly Process Costing' or MPC and we decided to design a system that does a couple of different things. The first thing we need to do is meet our goal of having good product cost. So we need to have processes defined and activities defined and to meet or satisfy the business requirements for information. But we still had the major roadblock that I described in the second phase of ABC --- we needed the plants to want the data. We couldn't have a system that only does process costing when the plants are organized functionally. We need both a process view and an organizational view, and we need the numbers to agree between the two views... So now we have two cost hierarchies. One looks a lot like an organizational chart --- so the plant manager can see all costs over time and they are separated by the folks who report to him. Meanwhile the production manager can see how costs are assigned across different production areas. Then we have the process view. The key difference is that the non-productive areas, like for example maintenance, aren't visible because these costs are assigned to the productive area that they support.

With complex ABC models falling out of favor, and the focus shifting from detailed product costs --- the result of two-stage cost allocations --- to process costs --- the result of cruder single-stage cost allocation, it might appear that ABC at Chrysler is at a pivotal point that could mark the "beginning of the end." However, managers were very quick to share with us internal documents that chart the outline of the new cost management system. We are not at liberty to describe the details of this system; however, materials that were presented at recent ABC practitioner meetings (e.g., CAM-I) indicate that the new generation of cost management systems features an integration of ABC product and process costing with a new performance measurement program. A key development of the new cost management system has been the uniting of cost data with performance measurement and management systems. In particular, a parallel effort to implement concepts from performance scorecards that link organizational strategy with performance measures has been integrated with the ongoing ABC program of improved product and process costing. Both of the new cost "views" are linked to performance goals. Moreover, the two MPC cost views are also integrated with a broader array of cost management tools and managerial practices, including: target costing, value engineering and engineering cost estimates, supply chain management and performance evaluation, and product profitability analysis. In short, cost management has become a corporate business process in its own right rather than simply a mathematical method or reporting style of plant analysts. However, the implementation of the "new" MPC system has not been without its pitfalls --- though perhaps not those that have been predicted by the business press, which has focused on the dislocation brought about by the marriage of Daimler-Benz and Chrysler:

I thought for sure our project would have been in jeopardy when [our manager, who championed ABC] went to Germany and a German replaced him... because the view that standardized processes are desirable is not prevalent in the Daimler culture. But this didn't come to pass. With MPC we are still fighting the classic barriers to change --- [managers complain that they] ... 'don't have time to learn a new process and nobody is asking for this, so there is no need for it.' ..It's not about costing per se... or any managerial practice. It's about organizational change. The latest one in finance is EVA [Economic Value Added]. We've really struggled with taking this conceptual idea, putting it into practice and getting something out of it.

4. COMMON THEMES, UNCOMMON CHALLENGES

In conducting interviews with managers who have been involved with ABC and with cost management practices at GM and Chrysler for more than a decade and for much of their professional lives, we are struck by recurring and common themes.

A dominant theme of the current manifestation of ABC is that of the present challenge being fundamentally that of integration ---

- integration of ABC with a broader array of cost management practices,
- integration of ABC, which was developed initially around a business process view with a more traditional organizational reporting view,
- integration of ABC with corporate strategy and planning, through performance measurement approaches such as performance scorecards; and finally,
- technical integration using data warehousing and systems architectures to address concerns about system maintenance and data integrity.

These themes are recognizable in the Chrysler Group and in the areas of GM where ABC has thrived.

A second theme that emerges in both firms is the importance of key individuals in promoting and championing management initiatives. At GM, the untimely death in 1993 of a key proponent of ABC and the retirement in 1995 of the another senior manager who had been involved with ABC since its inception reduced the visibility of ABC in core manufacturing operations. Similarly, the spin-off of many noncore plants with the formation of Delphi Automotive, removed a critical group of ABC users who were most supportive of ABC as an important management tool. Finally, severe downsizing pressures at the plant level caused many ABC development teams to be disbanded in the mid 1990's

A third theme, which was implicated directly in the form that ABC adaptation and evolution took, is that information systems are costly --- costly to create, and perhaps more subtle, very costly to maintain --- and that for their benefits to be realized, the intended users must believe that the effort of learning new methods is warranted. Both firms struggled to make ABC model development and maintenance easier and to make data from other operational systems more accessible. As a GM manager noted, "The process was so cumbersome to the plants that they did not want to spend the energy and resources to do it. We might have had a chance at making ABC "stick" as a plant system if we'd found an easier way to support it." At Chrysler, several adaptations of ABC were explicitly aimed at reducing the time to develop and maintain the ABC model, even at the expense of perceived cost accuracy. The manager at GM was quick to add however that he was not hopeful about a technical solution existing... "I've seen most of the ABC software out there, and the key thing is ABC is still a very specialized activity. It's not easy to really do ABC in an organization that has been entrenched in the simplicity of labor-based processes. We have to find an easier way to do it and we have to make sure that we are identifying how the organization can use the data to more effectively do their jobs." Chrysler confronted similar issues about the demand for ABC data when they realized that the functionally organized plants were unprepared to digest the new "process view" of costs, in part because it conflicted with performance evaluation and control systems.

A fourth theme, which has been the underlying thesis of this book, is that both organizations are far from any hoped for new equilibrium of cost management practices. Indeed, after fifteen years of nearly constant adaptation and evolution of ABC, we speculate that the entire notion of "normal" routine management practices is a myth. Moreover, the replacement of objectives in the 1980's of developing a system that would provide more "accurate product costs" by a concern in 2000 for simplicity, ease of maintenance and linkage with performance management and control practices looks hauntingly cyclical, suggesting that even the notion of change representing progress is a myth. For example, the new "hybrid" MPC system at Chrysler bears a strong resemblance to the early precursors to ABC at General Motors, such as the "factored piece rate system" that we describe in Chapter 3

A final theme, takes us full circle to one of our initial hypotheses about ABC implementation. The managers we talked with during these most recent interviews were very clear in their summing up of what they had learned about ABC implementation. That is, that even though ABC focuses on changes to the cost and performance management system, the issue isn't about cost and performance measurement per se. When, asked whether the focus on the innovation was critical, a senior manager said, "No, pick one. The real issue is about managing organizational change. Right now, we are dealing with the same kinds of issues regarding EVA implementation [economic value added].

Organizations of all types and sizes face very similar issues regarding how to successfully implement management innovations. We conclude by prescribing that much more attention be paid to learning about the change management process, before investing millions in the latest great idea.

APPENDIX 2: ORIGINAL ABC DEVELOPER'S SURVEY

SURVEY OF ACTIVITY BASED COSTING IMPLEMENTATION

Professor Shannon W. Anderson
University of Michigan School of Business Administration

Professor S. Mark Young
University of Southern California School of Accounting

A cost analysis method called activity based costing (ABC) has been implemented in the plant where you work. This implementation was part of your company's implementation of ABC.

This survey is part of a collaborative research effort between Chrysler and professors from the University of Michigan and the University of Southern California. The objective of the research is to understand the factors that influence the success of management initiatives, like ABC, so that the company can be more effective in introducing them in the future.

The researchers have signed a confidentiality agreement with Chrysler's top managers and will not be allowed to divulge any information that top management determines is proprietary. In addition, your individual survey responses will be treated as confidential and will not be provided to management. The researchers will average your responses with those of other individuals in the plant and, in some cases, with those of individuals from other plants before presenting their findings to management. *The information will not be used in any way to evaluate the performance of a plant, an individual, or any groups of individuals.* This high level of confidentiality is provided so that you will feel free to respond honestly and openly to all of the questions that follow.

Please answer all of the questions so that we can develop a complete database. If you would like to add comments or explain any of your answers, you may use the last page of the survey. Thank you for your participation in this research project.

Shannon W. Anderson
Assistant Professor of Accounting &
Arthur Andersen Faculty Fellow
University of Michigan

S. Mark Young
Associate Professor of Accounting
University of Southern California

I. ABC WORK EXPERIENCE

The following questions ask for information about your work on activity based costing.

1. Did you work on the <u>first</u> ABC model for this plant? Yes _____ No _____

2. Were you involved with updating the ABC model? Yes _____ No _____

3. When (approximately) were you involved with ABC? From: ____ mo. ____ yr. To: ____ mo. ____ yr.

4. During this period, approximately what portion of your time was spent on ABC:

    ___ 100% ___ 75% ___ 50% ___ 25% ___ less than 10%

5. If you were not full-time, please describe your other job responsibilities:

   _____

   _____

   _____

   _____

6. Including yourself, how many people worked on ABC during this period? _____

7. List the people, if any, who worked on ABC with you. Include people from the plant as well as liaisons and outside consultants (if any) who worked with you. Indicate each team member's affiliation and their official time commitment to developing the ABC model (place an 'X' in all applicable columns):

Name of ABC Team Members	Local Plant	Division/ Corporate	External Consultant	100%	75%	50%	25%	<10%

8. Name the ABC team member, if any, who was the official leader for the team: _____

9. Name the ABC team member who *you believe* provided the most leadership for the team: _____

   _____

10. Name the person (if any) to whom the ABC team reported and give his or her job title.
    Name: _____ Job Title: _____

11. Name the person to whom *you personally* reported while you worked on ABC and give his or her job title. Name: ___
    _____ Job Title: _____

12. Name the person *in the plant* who was the 'champion' for ABC and give his or her job title. This individual may not be the person to whom you reported. Please name the individual who *you believe* provided critical support for the project. If no such person existed write 'NONE'.
Name: _____ Job Title:_____

13. What version of the ABC Profit Manager software was used? _____

14. Have you ever attended a corporate ABC Users Group meeting?   Yes _____   No _____

15. How many times has the original ABC model been updated? _____

16. How frequently is the ABC model updated at this plant? (check one: 'X')

Quarterly _____ Every 6 months _____ Every year _____

The model has been updated, but is updated only on an as-needed basis _____

There are no plans to update _____   I do not know _____

II. ABC WORK ORGANIZATION AND ROLE OF RESPONDENT

Please answer the following questions by circling the appropriate number using the scale below.

1	2	3	4	5
Strongly Disagree	Disagree	Neither agree nor disagree	Agree	Strongly Agree

It is possible that you do not have the necessary information to form an opinion on every aspect of activity based costing. In these cases we have added the response "N/A" to represent the response "Not Applicable." Use this category if you have no information on this topic. Use the response "3" if you are informed, but have no opinion on the topic.

A. ABC Team

The following section asks questions about how the ABC team organized the work of ABC implementation and the role(s) that you played on the team. **If you were the only person who worked on the ABC model for this plant, please go to Section B on page 4.**

DO YOU AGREE OR DISAGREE?

1.	There was a strong feeling of camaraderie among ABC team members.	1 2 3 4 5 N/A
2.	The ABC team had clear understanding of its work objectives.	1 2 3 4 5 N/A
3.	I was very involved with analyzing the ABC costs from the ABC model and comparing them with the costs of the traditional model.	1 2 3 4 5 N/A
4.	I feel little loyalty to the ABC team.	1 2 3 4 5 N/A
5.	As part of the ABC team, I was responsible for a specific component of the ABC model.	1 2 3 4 5 N/A
6.	ABC team members were knowledgeable about the plant's information systems.	1 2 3 4 5 N/A
7.	Each member of the ABC team had a clear idea of the team's goals.	1 2 3 4 5 N/A

Please answer the following questions by circling the appropriate number using the scale below

1	2	3	4	5
Strongly Disagree	Disagree	Neither agree nor disagree	Agree	Strongly Agree

It is possible that you do not have the necessary information to form an opinion on every aspect of activity based costing. In these cases we have added the response "N/A" to represent the response "Not Applicable." Use this category if you have no information on this topic. Use the response "3" if you are informed, but have no opinion on the topic.

DO YOU AGREE OR DISAGREE?

8. Before being assigned to the ABC project, ABC team members were well known by many people in different areas of the plant.   1 2 3 4 5 N/A

9. When a disagreement arose between ABC team members everyone tried to find a workable solution.   1 2 3 4 5 N/A

10. ABC team members were knowledgeable about the traditional cost system.   1 2 3 4 5 N/A

11. I looked forward to working with ABC team members each day.   1 2 3 4 5 N/A

12. I was very involved with conducting interviews with employees.   1 2 3 4 5 N/A

13. I am proud to work on the ABC team.   1 2 3 4 5 N/A

14. Members of the ABC team were skilled computer users.   1 2 3 4 5 N/A

15. Members of the ABC team had very different backgrounds.   1 2 3 4 5 N/A

16. On the ABC team, everyone's opinions were heard.   1 2 3 4 5 N/A

17. The ABC team divided its tasks so that each team member had a few tasks for which they were solely responsible.   1 2 3 4 5 N/A

18. Everyone on the ABC team clearly understood the team's objectives.   1 2 3 4 5 N/A

19. I was very involved with the process of identifying 'activities' for the ABC model.   1 2 3 4 5 N/A

20. ABC team members were knowledgeable about the plant's production processes.   1 2 3 4 5 N/A

21. There were differences of opinion among members of the ABC team.   1 2 3 4 5 N/A

22. When a decision was required, every member of the ABC team was involved.   1 2 3 4 5 N/A

23. A dominant member of the team usually imposed his or her solution when there was disagreement among ABC team members.   1 2 3 4 5 N/A

24. The ABC team set its own schedule for completing the ABC model.   1 2 3 4 5 N/A

25. Disagreements were rare among members of the ABC team.   1 2 3 4 5 N/A

26. When I was on the ABC team I felt that I was really a part of the group.   1 2 3 4 5 N/A

27. I was very involved in selecting cost drivers for the ABC model.   1 2 3 4 5 N/A

28. Some members of the ABC team were afraid to speak up when they disagreed with the group's decision.   1 2 3 4 5 N/A

29. I can achieve my career goals at the same time as the ABC team achieves its goals.   1 2 3 4 5 N/A

30. If a disagreement arose between ABC team members, the issue was dealt with in an open fashion.   1 2 3 4 5 N/A

Please answer the following questions by circling the appropriate number using the scale below

1	2	3	4	5
Strongly Disagree	Disagree	Neither agree nor disagree	Agree	Strongly Agree

It is possible that you do not have the necessary information to form an opinion on every aspect of activity based costing. In these cases we have added the response "N/A" to represent the response "Not Applicable." Use this category if you have no information on this topic. Use the response "3" if you are informed, but have no opinion on the topic.

DO YOU AGREE OR DISAGREE?

31. Members of the ABC team varied widely in their skills and abilities.   1 2 3 4 5 N/A

32. I was very involved in collecting quantitative data for the ABC model.   1 2 3 4 5 N/A

33. The members of the ABC team respected one another.   1 2 3 4 5 N/A

B. Individual's ABC Work Experience

The following section asks questions about your experiences working on ABC.

1. The work I did on ABC was extremely meaningful to me.   1 2 3 4 5 N/A

2. I know ABC team members from other plants well enough to call them if I have a question that I believe they can answer.   1 2 3 4 5 N/A

3. I am a skilled user of PROFIT MANAGER.   1 2 3 4 5 N/A

4. Work on ABC requires the ability to work closely with other people.   1 2 3 4 5 N/A

5. My work on ABC had a visible effect on this plant.   1 2 3 4 5 N/A

6. I had access to the equipment and materials that I needed to complete my work on ABC.   1 2 3 4 5 N/A

7. Before being assigned to the ABC project, I was well known by many people in different areas of the plant.   1 2 3 4 5 N/A

8. Involvement with ABC will enhance my future career opportunities.   1 2 3 4 5 N/A

9. I am a skilled user of at least one piece of database software for personal computers (for example, Paradox, Fox Pro, D-Base, Microsoft Access).   1 2 3 4 5 N/A

10. I have not had enough training to perform my work on ABC well.   1 2 3 4 5 N/A

11. The external consultant (if any) provided adequate support to this plant's ABC team.   1 2 3 4 5 N/A

12. Managers of the plant were involved in determining how their departmental expenses were allocated to activities and products.   1 2 3 4 5 N/A

13. As I performed my tasks on ABC, I could see the contribution I was making.   1 2 3 4 5 N/A

14. Most of the tasks associated with my work on the ABC team were well defined.   1 2 3 4 5 N/A

15. This plant's ABC model uses a great deal of information that is downloaded from other systems.   1 2 3 4 5 N/A

16. ABC is a passing fad at this company.   1 2 3 4 5 N/A

17. My work on the ABC team was extremely challenging.   1 2 3 4 5 N/A

Please answer the following questions by circling the appropriate number using the scale below

1	2	3	4	5
Strongly Disagree	Disagree	Neither agree nor disagree	Agree	Strongly Agree

It is possible that you do not have the necessary information to form an opinion on every aspect of activity based costing. In these cases we have added the response "N/A" to represent the response "Not Applicable." Use this category if you have no information on this topic. Use the response "3" if you are informed, but have no opinion on the topic.

DO YOU AGREE OR DISAGREE?

18. A lot of people will be affected by how I do my job on ABC.   1 2 3 4 5 N/A

19. A high level of computer knowledge increases one's effectiveness in building ABC models.   1 2 3 4 5 N/A

20. My skill developing ABC models could be improved.   1 2 3 4 5 N/A

21. We experienced problems downloading data from the plant's information systems into the ABC model.   1 2 3 4 5 N/A

22. I found PROFIT MANAGER to be flexible for my purposes.   1 2 3 4 5 N/A

23. I, or my ABC team members, contacted ABC teams from other plants when questions arose about how to proceed with our work.   1 2 3 4 5 N/A

24. Management at this plant viewed the external consultant (if any) as the leader of the ABC initiative.   1 2 3 4 5 N/A

25. I felt personally accountable for the timely completion of the ABC model.   1 2 3 4 5 N/A

26. Working on ABC gave me the opportunity to contribute something worthwhile to this plant.   1 2 3 4 5 N/A

27. Errors in existing information systems made building the ABC model very difficult.   1 2 3 4 5 N/A

28. Before being assigned to the ABC project, I was very knowledgable about the traditional accounting system.   1 2 3 4 5 N/A

29. While working on ABC, I knew whether my work was satisfactory.   1 2 3 4 5 N/A

30. Being selected to work on ABC indicated that management believes that I have strong promotion opportunities.   1 2 3 4 5 N/A

31. I am a skilled user of at least one piece of spreadsheet software for personal computers (for example, Lotus 1-2-3, Quattro Pro or Excel).   1 2 3 4 5 N/A

32. The external consultant (if any) made many of the major decisions about this plant's ABC model.   1 2 3 4 5 N/A

33. I feel a very strong commitment to this plant's ABC effort.   1 2 3 4 5 N/A

34. When individuals involved with ABC meet with local managers, they receive improvement suggestions from the managers.   1 2 3 4 5 N/A

35. Support for implementing ABC in this company is widespread.   1 2 3 4 5 N/A

36. I, or my ABC team members, communicated with ABC teams from other plants.   1 2 3 4 5 N/A

37. I am a skilled user of at least one piece of word processing software for personal computers (for example, WordPerfect, Word, Volkswriter).   1 2 3 4 5 N/A

Please answer the following questions by circling the appropriate number using the scale below

1	2	3	4	5
Strongly Disagree	Disagree	Neither agree nor disagree	Agree	Strongly Agree

It is possible that you do not have the necessary information to form an opinion on every aspect of activity based costing. In these cases we have added the response "N/A" to represent the response "Not Applicable." Use this category if you have no information on this topic. Use the response "3" if you are informed, but have no opinion on the topic.

DO YOU AGREE OR DISAGREE?

38. I set my own schedule for completing the ABC model.   1 2 3 4 5 N/A

39. The future of this plant will be affected by how well I do my job on ABC.   1 2 3 4 5 N/A

40. I have all of the skills I need in order to do my job on ABC.   1 2 3 4 5 N/A

41. ABC implementation is easier if the union and management have a good relationship.   1 2 3 4 5 N/A

42. I volunteered to work on ABC.   1 2 3 4 5 N/A

43. Most of the data that was needed to develop a good ABC model was readily available.   1 2 3 4 5 N/A

44. Managers of the plant were involved in defining the plant's activity centers.   1 2 3 4 5 N/A

45. While working on ABC, I knew what was expected of me.   1 2 3 4 5 N/A

46. The local union was aware of the ABC initiative at this plant.   1 2 3 4 5 N/A

47. I found PROFIT MANAGER easy to use.   1 2 3 4 5 N/A

48. Work on ABC requires the ability to cooperate with people from many different functional areas.   1 2 3 4 5 N/A

49. Before being assigned to the ABC project, I was very knowledgable about the production processes in this plant.   1 2 3 4 5 N/A

50. I had access to the people who I needed to talk to during my work on ABC.   1 2 3 4 5 N/A

51. Most managers of this plant are capable of using ABC data to reduce costs.   1 2 3 4 5 N/A

52. I believe that ABC can help this plant.   1 2 3 4 5 N/A

53. An ABC assignment is likely to hurt someone's career.   1 2 3 4 5 N/A

54. This company's top managers have provided visible support for the ABC initiative.   1 2 3 4 5 N/A

55. While working on ABC, I had too much work to do everything well.   1 2 3 4 5 N/A

56. Most managers of this plant have been supportive of the ABC team's work.   1 2 3 4 5 N/A

57. I found it easy to get PROFIT MANAGER to do what I wanted it to do.   1 2 3 4 5 N/A

58. I felt responsible for the success of ABC.   1 2 3 4 5 N/A

59. The ABC effort received adequate support from an ABC liaison.   1 2 3 4 5 N/A

60. The ABC initiative was staffed adequately to insure completion of the task in the time allotted.   1 2 3 4 5 N/A

61. The local union was involved in decisions that affected the ABC model.   1 2 3 4 5 N/A

Please answer the following questions by circling the appropriate number using the scale below

1	2	3	4	5
Strongly Disagree	Disagree	Neither agree nor disagree	Agree	Strongly Agree

It is possible that you do not have the necessary information to form an opinion on every aspect of activity based costing. In these cases we have added the response "N/A" to represent the response "Not Applicable." Use this category if you have no information on this topic. Use the response "3" if you are informed, but have no opinion on the topic.

DO YOU AGREE OR DISAGREE?

62. Building the ABC system was mentally demanding.　　　　1　2　3　4　5　N/A

63. The plant's information systems generally provide data that is accurate and up to date.　　　　1　2　3　4　5　N/A

64. Support for implementing ABC in this company comes from both the operating and finance groups.　　　　1　2　3　4　5　N/A

65. The local union is receptive to the concept of ABC.　　　　1　2　3　4　5　N/A

66. The corporate finance and accounting group provided support for implementing ABC in this company.　　　　1　2　3　4　5　N/A

III. ABC ASSESSMENT

The following questions ask for your assessment of ABC implementation at this plant and your assessment of the usefulness of data from the ABC model.

1. Data from the ABC model provides an accurate assessment of costs in this plant.　　　　1　2　3　4　5　N/A

2. I was surprised by the data from the ABC model.　　　　1　2　3　4　5　N/A

3. The managers of this plant are knowledgeable about the theory of ABC.　　　　1　2　3　4　5　N/A

4. In general ABC is a good thing for this company.　　　　1　2　3　4　5　N/A

5. Data from the ABC model is used only for special cost studies.　　　　1　2　3　4　5　N/A

6. The ABC costs do not seem reasonable to me based on what I know about this plant.　　　　1　2　3　4　5　N/A

7. Information from the ABC model has had a noticeable positive impact on this plant.　　　　1　2　3　4　5　N/A

8. Overall, ABC implementation has been a worthwhile experience for this plant.　　　　1　2　3　4　5　N/A

9. The managers at this plant understand the importance of ABC.　　　　1　2　3　4　5　N/A

10. Data from the ABC model is used to replace traditional costs in most instances where cost information is required.　　　　1　2　3　4　5　N/A

11. Despite the implementation challenges, I am convinced that ABC is the right tool for helping us manage costs in this company.　　　　1　2　3　4　5　N/A

12. Managers of this plant would like the ABC model to be updated more frequently.　　　　1　2　3　4　5　N/A

13. The managers of this plant are eager to get ABC data.　　　　1　2　3　4　5　N/A

14. Cost information from the ABC model is more accurate than that produced by the traditional cost system.　　　　1　2　3　4　5　N/A

Please answer the following questions by circling the appropriate number using the scale below

1	2	3	4	5
Strongly Disagree	Disagree	Neither agree nor disagree	Agree	Strongly Agree

It is possible that you do not have the necessary information to form an opinion on every aspect of activity based costing. In these cases we have added the response "N/A" to represent the response "Not Applicable." Use this category if you have no information on this topic. Use the response "3" if you are informed, but have no opinion on the topic.

DO YOU AGREE OR DISAGREE?

15. Supporting ABC is the right thing to do in this company.   1 2 3 4 5 N/A

16. Individuals from the corporate ABC Group are the only ones who care about this plant's ABC model.   1 2 3 4 5 N/A

17. If I were asked to decide whether this company should continue implementing ABC, I would vote to continue.   1 2 3 4 5 N/A

18. The results from the ABC model matched my intuition about costs of production.   1 2 3 4 5 N/A

19. Generally, managers prefer to use data from the traditional cost system rather than the ABC cost system.   1 2 3 4 5 N/A

20. ABC data didn't tell me anything that I didn't already know about costs in this plant.   1 2 3 4 5 N/A

21. The ABC model has not been used and has been 'gathering dust' since it was completed.   1 2 3 4 5 N/A

22. Overall, the benefits of ABC data outweigh the costs of installing a new system.   1 2 3 4 5 N/A

IV. WORK ENVIRONMENT

The following questions ask you about your feelings about your work and the work environment. Your responses to these questions will help us by providing a work context for your answers regarding ABC.

1. New management programs are introduced all the time in this plant.   1 2 3 4 5

2. The threat of layoffs or cutbacks to hourly workers is low.   1 2 3 4 5

3. I like things at work to be stable.   1 2 3 4 5

4. Getting authorization to hire new employees for this plant is difficult.   1 2 3 4 5

5. This plant runs three shifts and weekends on a regular basis.   1 2 3 4 5

6. Cost reduction is the most important objective in this plant.   1 2 3 4 5

7. I feel very little loyalty to this company.   1 2 3 4 5

8. I generally prefer to work as part of a team.   1 2 3 4 5

9. This plant has had major cutbacks and layoffs in recent years.   1 2 3 4 5

10. I get a great deal of satisfaction from doing a good job.   1 2 3 4 5

11. This plant produces virtually the same set of products every year.   1 2 3 4 5

12. In this plant, high performance is recognized and rewarded.   1 2 3 4 5

13. Changes in the way we work in this plant are needed.   1 2 3 4 5

Please answer the following questions by circling the appropriate number using the scale below

1	2	3	4	5
Strongly Disagree	Disagree	Neither agree nor disagree	Agree	Strongly Agree

It is possible that you do not have the necessary information to form an opinion on every aspect of activity based costing. In these cases we have added the response "N/A" to represent the response "Not Applicable." Use this category if you have no information on this topic. Use the response "3" if you are informed, but have no opinion on the topic.

DO YOU AGREE OR DISAGREE?

14.	My values and the values at this plant are quite similar.	1	2	3	4	5
15.	Most important decisions that affect this plant are made by the plant manager.	1	2	3	4	5
16.	The working environment at this plant changes constantly.	1	2	3	4	5
17.	Earning the respect of my peers through my performance is very important to me.	1	2	3	4	5
18.	This plant will be better off if we work as a team.	1	2	3	4	5
19.	The ability to reduce costs is rewarded in this plant.	1	2	3	4	5
20.	Relations between labor and management need to be improved at this plant.	1	2	3	4	5
21.	Cost reduction is not a major concern in this plant.	1	2	3	4	5
22.	This plant has had a lot of management turnover in recent years.	1	2	3	4	5
23.	This plant produces products that are very important to this company.	1	2	3	4	5
24.	When an important decision has to be made, employees are given the opportunity to provide input.	1	2	3	4	5
25.	There is no need for this plant to change the way it does things.	1	2	3	4	5
26.	I feel very little loyalty to this plant.	1	2	3	4	5
27.	Being respected by the people who I work with is more important than earning more money.	1	2	3	4	5
28.	At this plant the union and management have similar goals.	1	2	3	4	5
29.	This plant has difficulty getting authorization for new equipment.	1	2	3	4	5
30.	This plant is one of the most important manufacturing sites of this company.	1	2	3	4	5
31.	A changing work environment challenges me.	1	2	3	4	5
32.	This plant faces stiff competition from other plants in this company for business.	1	2	3	4	5
33.	I am proud to work for this plant.	1	2	3	4	5
34.	Obtaining greater job satisfaction is more important to me than making more money.	1	2	3	4	5
35.	Department managers at this plant are given authority to run their department as they see fit.	1	2	3	4	5
36.	Manufacturing processes at this plant change all the time.	1	2	3	4	5
37.	The threat of layoffs of management employees is high.	1	2	3	4	5
38.	I find that working as a member of a team increases my ability to perform effectively.	1	2	3	4	5
39.	This plant's cost reduction efforts are important to the company.	1	2	3	4	5
40.	My values and the values of this company are quite similar.	1	2	3	4	5

Please answer the following questions by circling the appropriate number using the scale below

1	2	3	4	5
Strongly Disagree	Disagree	Neither agree nor disagree	Agree	Strongly Agree

It is possible that you do not have the necessary information to form an opinion on every aspect of activity based costing. In these cases we have added the response "N/A" to represent the response "Not Applicable." Use this category if you have no information on this topic. Use the response "3" if you are informed, but have no opinion on the topic.

DO YOU AGREE OR DISAGREE?

41. In this plant, financial rewards are tied directly to performance.   1 2 3 4 5

42. Future demand for the products that this plant produces is uncertain.   1 2 3 4 5

43. I would like to see changes in plant policies and procedures.   1 2 3 4 5

44. Plant capacity utilization changes a great deal from year to year.   1 2 3 4 5

45. I am proud to work for this company.   1 2 3 4 5

46. The production equipment in this plant is unreliable and constantly breaks down.   1 2 3 4 5

47. I adapt well to a changing work environment.   1 2 3 4 5

48. In this plant, supervisors use suggestions that their employees make at work.   1 2 3 4 5

49. In this plant, high quality work increases my chances for a raise, a bonus, or a promotion.   1 2 3 4 5

50. Competitive pressures could cause this plant to close.   1 2 3 4 5

51. Most important decisions that affect this plant are made by people at the Division or Corporate.   1 2 3 4 5

52. This plant is critical for the success of this company.   1 2 3 4 5

53. This plant faces stiff competition from outside companies for business.   1 2 3 4 5

54. This plant's products are frequently modified by engineering changes.   1 2 3 4 5

55. Labor and management in this plant work well together.   1 2 3 4 5

56. We have difficulty getting authorization to hire replacements for employees who retire or leave this plant.   1 2 3 4 5

V. BACKGROUND INFORMATION

A. Education and Training

1.   Please place an 'X' beside the highest level of formal education that you attained:

High school diploma or equivalency exam   _____
Associates degree (2 years of college training)   _____
Bachelors degree (4 years of college training)   _____   Field   _____
Masters degree   _____   Field   _____
Other   _____   Field   _____

2.   Please place an 'X' beside the types of training that you have received in activity based costing. Then estimate the total hours that each course devoted to the topic of activity-based costing.

Types of Training   ABC hours
Degree-granting educational programs   _____   Total ABC class hours: _____
Non-degree courses offered by external provider _____   Total ABC class hours: _____
Non-degree courses offered by the company   _____   Total ABC class hours: _____
On the job training designed to teach about ABC _____
No training in ABC   _____

3.   Please place an 'X' beside the statement that <u>best</u> reflects your level of knowledge about the <u>general concepts</u> of activity based costing.

I've never heard of activity based costing   _____
I've heard of activity based costing, but I don't really know much about it   _____
I understand the basic concepts of activity based costing   _____
I know a great deal about activity based costing   _____
I consider myself an expert in activity based costing   _____

4.   Please place an 'X' beside the statement that <u>best</u> reflects your level of knowledge about the implementation of activity based costing at this plant.

I didn't know that this plant had an activity based costing system   _____
I'm aware that this plant has ABC, but I don't know much about it   _____
I'm aware that this plant has ABC and I have a general understanding of it   _____
I'm aware that this plant has ABC and know a great deal about it   _____
I am an expert in this plant's ABC system   _____

B. Work History

5.   How many years have you worked at this company? (round up to the nearest full year)   _____ yrs.

6.   How many years have you worked at this plant? (round up to the nearest full year)   _____ yrs.

7. Please provide information about the last two jobs that you have had. Begin with your current job and then provide information about the job that you held before that.

a) Current Job title _____ Department _____

Job Description: _____

Period of employment: FROM: _____ year   TO: _____ year

b) Job title _____ Department _____

Job Description: _____

Company Name (if different): _____

Period of employment: FROM: _____ year   TO: _____ year

166

If there is anything else that you would like to tell us about the plant or the ABC project, please use the space below.

Thank you for your assistance in helping us gather information about ABC implementation at this plant.

APPENDIX 3: Original Management Survey

MANAGEMENT SURVEY OF ACTIVITY BASED COSTING IMPLEMENTATION

Professor Shannon W. Anderson
University of Michigan School of Business Administration

Professor S. Mark Young
University of Southern California School of Accounting

A cost analysis system called activity based costing (ABC) was implemented in the plant where you work. This implementation was part of your company's implementation of ABC.

This survey is part of a collaborative research effort between Chrysler and professors from the University of Michigan and the University of Southern California. The objective of the research is to understand the factors that influence the success of management initiatives, like ABC, so that the company can be more effective in introducing them in the future.

The researchers have signed a confidentiality agreement with Chrysler's top managers and will not be allowed to divulge any information that top management determines is proprietary. In addition, your individual survey responses will be treated as confidential and will not be provided to management. The researchers will average your responses with those of other individuals in the plant and, in some cases, with those of individuals from other plants before presenting their findings to management. *The information will not be used in any way to evaluate the performance of a plant, an individual, or any groups of individuals.* This high level of confidentiality is provided so that you will feel free to respond honestly and openly to all of the questions that follow.

Please answer all of the questions so that we can develop a complete database. If you would like to add comments or explain any of your answers, you may use the last page of the survey. Thank you for your participation in this research project.

Shannon W. Anderson
Assistant Professor of Accounting &
Arthur Andersen Faculty Fellow
University of Michigan

S. Mark Young
Associate Professor of Accounting
University of Southern California

I. GENERAL QUESTIONS ABOUT ACTIVITY BASED COSTING

Please answer the following questions by circling the appropriate number using the scale below

1	2	3	4	5
Strongly Disagree	Disagree	Neither Agree nor disagree	Agree	Strongly Agree

It is possible that you do not have the necessary information to form an opinion on every aspect of activity based costing. In these cases we have added the response "N/A" to represent the response "Not Applicable." Use this category if you have no information on the topic. Use the response "3" if you are informed, but have no opinion on the topic.

The following questions ask for your opinions about the usefulness of ABC.

DO YOU AGREE OR DISAGREE?

1. ABC information causes me to think about problems differently at work.   1 2 3 4 5 N/A

2. ABC information is unlikely to affect the future of this plant.   1 2 3 4 5 N/A

3. Support for implementing ABC in this company is widespread.   1 2 3 4 5 N/A

4. The ABC implementations at other plants in this company have been successful.   1 2 3 4 5 N/A

5. When I first learned that ABC was being implemented at this plant I thought the costs would outweigh the benefits.   1 2 3 4 5 N/A

6. ABC data will help me manage the plant.   1 2 3 4 5 N/A

7. The work of the people who developed the ABC model has had a visible impact on this plant.   1 2 3 4 5 N/A

8. This plant's top managers have provided visible support for the ABC initiative.   1 2 3 4 5 N/A

9. I've read about ABC in articles in popular business periodicals.   1 2 3 4 5 N/A

10. From the first time I heard about ABC I knew that it was something that would help this plant.   1 2 3 4 5 N/A

11. ABC Cost information is more accurate than that produced by the traditional cost system.   1 2 3 4 5 N/A

12. A lot of people will be affected by how well the developers of the ABC model performed their job.   1 2 3 4 5 N/A

13. ABC is a waste of time and resources.   1 2 3 4 5 N/A

14. Support for implementing ABC in this company is coming primarily from the corporate finance and accounting group.   1 2 3 4 5 N/A

15. Other companies that have implemented ABC have found it to be very useful.   1 2 3 4 5 N/A

16. Before ABC was implemented, I was skeptical that it could help this plant.   1 2 3 4 5 N/A

17. I have no need for cost information in my job.   1 2 3 4 5 N/A

18. The future of this plant will be affected by how well the developers of the ABC model perform their job.   1 2 3 4 5 N/A

19. ABC is a popular management initiative that many companies are considering.   1 2 3 4 5 N/A

20. When I first learned about ABC, I was skeptical that it would be useful in my work.   1 2 3 4 5 N/A

Please answer the following questions by circling the appropriate number using the scale below

1	2	3	4	5
Strongly Disagree	Disagree	Neither Agree nor disagree	Agree	Strongly Agree

It is possible that you do not have the necessary information to form an opinion on every aspect of activity based costing. In these cases we have added the response "N/A" to represent the response "Not Applicable." Use this category if you have no information on the topic. Use the response "3" if you are informed, but have no opinion on the topic.

DO YOU AGREE OR DISAGREE?

21. This company's top managers have provided visible support for the ABC initiative. 1 2 3 4 5 N/A

22. The traditional cost system provided adequate information for me to do my job. 1 2 3 4 5 N/A

23. Support for implementing ABC in this company comes from both the manufacturing operations and finance groups. 1 2 3 4 5 N/A

24. The managers of this plant believe that the ABC project is important. 1 2 3 4 5 N/A

25. Other plants from this company that have implemented ABC have found it to be very useful. 1 2 3 4 5 N/A

26. ABC data will help managers run this plant better. 1 2 3 4 5 N/A

27. I feel a very strong personal commitment to this company's ABC implementation. 1 2 3 4 5 N/A

28. Product and process cost data are not useful in performing my job. 1 2 3 4 5 N/A

29. This company's top managers believe that ABC is important. 1 2 3 4 5 N/A

30. ABC is a passing fad in this company. 1 2 3 4 5 N/A

II. YOUR INVOLVEMENT WITH ACTIVITY BASED COSTING

The following section asks questions about your involvement with this plant's ABC implementation. You are also asked to assess the extent to which other managers, members of the union, and external consultants were involved with ABC implementation.

1. I received adequate training in the theory of how ABC works. 1 2 3 4 5 N/A

2. I was involved in the selection of individuals to work on the ABC model. 1 2 3 4 5 N/A

3. An external consultant made many of the decisions about this plant's ABC model. 1 2 3 4 5 N/A

4. The local union was aware of the ABC model as it was being developed. 1 2 3 4 5 N/A

5. Most managers of the plant were involved in determining how their departmental expenses were allocated to activities and products. 1 2 3 4 5 N/A

6. I have a clear understanding of how to use ABC data in my job. 1 2 3 4 5 N/A

7. My opinion was sought when 'activity centers' were defined for the ABC model. 1 2 3 4 5 N/A

8. The developers of the ABC model conducted periodic meetings with management to review their work. 1 2 3 4 5 N/A

9. I have all of the skills I need in order to use ABC data effectively in my job. 1 2 3 4 5 N/A

Please answer the following questions by circling the appropriate number using the scale below

1	2	3	4	5
Strongly Disagree	Disagree	Neither Agree nor disagree	Agree	Strongly Agree

It is possible that you do not have the necessary information to form an opinion on every aspect of activity based costing. In these cases we have added the response "N/A" to represent the response "Not Applicable." Use this category if you have no information on the topic. Use the response "3" if you are informed, but have no opinion on the topic.

DO YOU AGREE OR DISAGREE?

10. My opinion was sought about how costs from my department should be allocated to activities and products.   1 2 3 4 5 N/A

11. An external consultant was in an 'advising' role and was only involved with decisions about the ABC model when assistance was necessary.   1 2 3 4 5 N/A

12. The local union is receptive to the concept of ABC.   1 2 3 4 5 N/A

13. I was shown prototypes of the ABC model as it was developed.   1 2 3 4 5 N/A

14. Using ABC data is mentally demanding.   1 2 3 4 5 N/A

15. I was interviewed by the developers of the ABC model about my job.   1 2 3 4 5 N/A

16. The developers of the ABC model presented a formal analysis of the ABC data when the system was completed.   1 2 3 4 5 N/A

17. Most managers of this plant are capable of using ABC data to reduce costs.   1 2 3 4 5 N/A

18. Before starting, the developers of the ABC model presented a plan to the managers of this plant for collecting data and a time schedule for completing the ABC model   1 2 3 4 5 N/A

19. The developers of the ABC model were given clear objectives by management.   1 2 3 4 5 N/A

20. This plant's managers understand ABC.   1 2 3 4 5 N/A

21. I was given the opportunity to tell the developers of the ABC model what cost information I need to do my job.   1 2 3 4 5 N/A

22. The local union was involved in decisions that affected the ABC model.   1 2 3 4 5 N/A

23. The managers of this plant are knowledgeable about the theory of ABC.   1 2 3 4 5 N/A

24. An external consultant was the leader of this plant's ABC initiative.   1 2 3 4 5 N/A

25. I was given the opportunity to tell the developers of the ABC model what types of reports that I would like to receive from the cost system.   1 2 3 4 5 N/A

26. Most people who work in my department understand ABC.   1 2 3 4 5 N/A

27. The developers of the ABC model kept me informed during the ABC model development.   1 2 3 4 5 N/A

28. Local union representatives attended most of the presentations about ABC and the development of the ABC model.   1 2 3 4 5 N/A

29. I formally reviewed the ABC model at several points during its development.   1 2 3 4 5 N/A

30. When the developers of the ABC model met with local managers, they received suggestions from the managers.   1 2 3 4 5 N/A

III. ABC MODEL DEVELOPMENT

Please answer the following questions by circling the appropriate number using the scale below

1	2	3	4	5
Strongly Disagree	Disagree	Neither Agree nor disagree	Agree	Strongly Agree

It is possible that you do not have the necessary information to form an opinion on every aspect of activity based costing. In these cases we have added the response "N/A" to represent the response "Not Applicable." Use this category if you have no information on the topic. Use the response "3" if you are informed, but have no opinion on the topic.

The following section asks your opinions about the requirements for ABC implementation and the adequacy of resources that were available to the people who developed this plant's ABC model.

DO YOU AGREE OR DISAGREE?

1. Building an ABC model is mentally challenging. 1 2 3 4 5 N/A

2. The people who developed the ABC model had the equipment and materials needed to do their job. 1 2 3 4 5 N/A

3. The people who developed the ABC model were adequately trained to do their jobs well. 1 2 3 4 5 N/A

4. Being selected to work on developing the ABC model is an indication that you have strong promotion opportunities at this plant. 1 2 3 4 5 N/A

5. Work on ABC requires cooperation with people from many different functional areas. 1 2 3 4 5 N/A

6. The people who worked on the ABC model are some of the best employees of this plant. 1 2 3 4 5 N/A

7. ABC implementation is easier if the union and management have a good relationship. 1 2 3 4 5 N/A

8. Most of the data required for a good ABC model was readily available in this plant. 1 2 3 4 5 N/A

9. Effective ABC development requires a high level of computer knowledge. 1 2 3 4 5 N/A

10. The people who developed the ABC model had access to the people from whom they needed to get information. 1 2 3 4 5 N/A

11. The people who developed the ABC model had the necessary social and human relations skills to perform their job well. 1 2 3 4 5 N/A

12. Involvement with ABC enhances an individual's future career opportunities. 1 2 3 4 5 N/A

13. The ABC development project was adequately staffed to insure completion of the task in the time allotted. 1 2 3 4 5 N/A

14. Work on ABC is so simple that virtually anybody could handle it with little training. 1 2 3 4 5 N/A

15. The plant's information systems generally provide data that is accurate and up to date. 1 2 3 4 5 N/A

16. The people who developed the ABC model received adequate encouragement and support from this plant's management team. 1 2 3 4 5 N/A

17. The information systems of this plant contain many data errors. 1 2 3 4 5 N/A

IV. THE ABC IMPLEMENTATION PROCESS

Please answer the following questions by circling the appropriate number using the scale below

1	2	3	4	5
Strongly Disagree	Disagree	Neither Agree nor disagree	Agree	Strongly Agree

It is possible that you do not have the necessary information to form an opinion on every aspect of activity based costing. In these cases we have added the response "N/A" to represent the response "Not Applicable." Use this category if you have no information on the topic. Use the response "3" if you are informed, but have no opinion on the topic.

The following questions ask your assessment of ABC implementation at this plant and your assessment of the usefulness of data from the ABC model.

DO YOU AGREE OR DISAGREE?

1. Data from the ABC model provides an accurate assessment of costs in this plant.   1   2   3   4   5   N/A

2. I was surprised by the data from the ABC model.   1   2   3   4   5   N/A

3. In general ABC is a good thing for this company.   1   2   3   4   5   N/A

4. People who work in my department are responsible for helping to reduce costs.   1   2   3   4   5   N/A

5. Using ABC data will improve my job performance.   1   2   3   4   5   N/A

6. Data from the ABC model is used only for special cost studies.   1   2   3   4   5   N/A

7. I am reluctant to use ABC data in place of costs from the traditional cost system.   1   2   3   4   5   N/A

8. The ABC costs do not seem reasonable to me based on what I know about this plant.   1   2   3   4   5   N/A

9. Information from the ABC model has had a noticeable positive impact on this plant.   1   2   3   4   5   N/A

10. Overall, ABC implementation has been a worthwhile experience for this plant.   1   2   3   4   5   N/A

11. I expect the people who work in my department to use ABC data to reduce costs.   1   2   3   4   5   N/A

12. Data from the ABC model is used to replace traditional costs in most instances where cost information is required.   1   2   3   4   5   N/A

13. ABC data is not likely to enhance my effectiveness on the job.   1   2   3   4   5   N/A

14. Despite the implementation challenges, I am convinced that ABC is the right tool for helping us manage costs in this company.   1   2   3   4   5   N/A

15. Managers of this plant would like the ABC model to be updated more frequently.   1   2   3   4   5   N/A

16. The managers of this plant are eager to get ABC data.   1   2   3   4   5   N/A

17. Supporting ABC is the right thing to do in this company.   1   2   3   4   5   N/A

18. Individuals from the corporate ABC Group are the only ones who care about this plant's ABC model.   1   2   3   4   5   N/A

19. If I were asked to decide whether this company should continue implementing ABC, I would vote to continue.   1   2   3   4   5   N/A

20. The results from the ABC model matched my intuition about costs of production.   1   2   3   4   5   N/A

21. I am responsible for cost reduction in this plant.   1   2   3   4   5   N/A

Please answer the following questions by circling the appropriate number using the scale below

1	2	3	4	5
Strongly Disagree	Disagree	Neither Agree nor disagree	Agree	Strongly Agree

It is possible that you do not have the necessary information to form an opinion on every aspect of activity based costing. In these cases we have added the response "N/A" to represent the response "Not Applicable." Use this category if you have no information on the topic. Use the response "3" if you are informed, but have no opinion on the topic.

DO YOU AGREE OR DISAGREE?

22.	People who work in my department have used ABC data in their jobs.	1	2	3	4	5	N/A
23.	ABC data didn't tell me anything that I didn't already know about costs in this plant.	1	2	3	4	5	N/A
24.	The ABC model has not been used and has been 'gathering dust' since it was completed.	1	2	3	4	5	N/A
25.	I am expected to use ABC data to reduce costs.	1	2	3	4	5	N/A
26.	Overall, the benefits of ABC data outweigh the costs of installing a new system.	1	2	3	4	5	N/A
27.	I have used ABC data to analyze the costs of the department that I manage.	1	2	3	4	5	N/A

V. PLANT WORK ENVIRONMENT

The following questions ask you about your feelings about your work and the work environment. Your responses to these questions will help us by providing a work context for your answers regarding ABC.

1.	I find that working as a member of a team increases my ability to perform effectively.	1	2	3	4	5
2.	My values and the values at this plant are quite similar.	1	2	3	4	5
3.	Changes in the way we work in this plant are needed.	1	2	3	4	5
4.	A changing work environment challenges me.	1	2	3	4	5
5.	In this plant, supervisors use suggestions that their employees make at work.	1	2	3	4	5
6.	I get a great deal of satisfaction from doing a good job.	1	2	3	4	5
7.	This plant produces virtually the same set of products every year.	1	2	3	4	5
8.	In this plant, high performance is recognized and rewarded.	1	2	3	4	5
9.	When an important decision has to be made, employees are given the opportunity to provide input.	1	2	3	4	5
10.	I would like to see changes in plant policies and procedures.	1	2	3	4	5
11.	Relations between labor and management need to be improved at this plant.	1	2	3	4	5
12	This plant faces competition from other plants in this company for business.	1	2	3	4	5
13.	In this plant, high quality work increases my chances for a raise, a bonus, or a promotion.	1	2	3	4	5
14.	This plant runs three shifts and weekends on a regular basis.	1	2	3	4	5
15.	Manufacturing processes at this plant change all the time.	1	2	3	4	5

174

Please answer the following questions by circling the appropriate number using the scale below

1	2	3	4	5
Strongly Disagree	Disagree	Neither Agree nor disagree	Agree	Strongly Agree

DO YOU AGREE OR DISAGREE?

16. I feel very little loyalty to this company.   1 2 3 4 5

17. Being respected by the people who I work with is more important than earning more money.   1 2 3 4 5

18. This plant has difficulty getting authorization for new equipment.   1 2 3 4 5

19. Cost reduction is not a major concern in this plant.   1 2 3 4 5

20. This plant is critical for the success of this company.   1 2 3 4 5

21. I like things at work to be stable.   1 2 3 4 5

22. This plant has had a lot of management turnover in recent years.   1 2 3 4 5

23. Getting authorization to hire new employees for this plant is difficult.   1 2 3 4 5

24. This plant is one of the most important manufacturing sites of this company.   1 2 3 4 5

25. I am proud to work for this plant.   1 2 3 4 5

26. At this plant the union and management have similar goals.   1 2 3 4 5

27. Obtaining greater job satisfaction is more important to me than making more money.   1 2 3 4 5

28. There is no need for this plant to change the way it does things.   1 2 3 4 5

29. My values and the values of this company are quite similar.   1 2 3 4 5

30. This plant faces stiff competition from outside companies for business.   1 2 3 4 5

31. The ability to reduce costs is rewarded in this plant.   1 2 3 4 5

32. Most important decisions that affect this plant are made by people at division or corporate offices.   1 2 3 4 5

33. I adapt well to a changing work environment.   1 2 3 4 5

34. Most important decisions that affect this plant are made by the plant manager.   1 2 3 4 5

35. The production equipment in this plant is unreliable and constantly breaks down.   1 2 3 4 5

36. The threat of layoffs or cutbacks to hourly workers is low.   1 2 3 4 5

37. This plant's cost reduction efforts are important to the company.   1 2 3 4 5

38. We have difficulty getting authorization to hire replacements for employees who retire or leave this plant.   1 2 3 4 5

39. This plant will be better off if we work as a team.   1 2 3 4 5

40. Labor and management in this plant work well together.   1 2 3 4 5

41. Plant capacity utilization changes a great deal from year to year.   1 2 3 4 5

42. Competitive pressures could cause this plant to close.   1 2 3 4 5

43. I feel very little loyalty to this plant.   1 2 3 4 5

Please answer the following questions by circling the appropriate number using the scale below

1	2	3	4	5
Strongly Disagree	Disagree	Neither Agree nor disagree	Agree	Strongly Agree

DO YOU AGREE OR DISAGREE?

44. This plant produces products that have a major influence on this company's profitability.   1 2 3 4 5

45. Future demand for the products that this plant produces is uncertain.   1 2 3 4 5

46. Earning the respect of my peers through my performance is very important to me.   1 2 3 4 5

47. I generally prefer to work as part of a team.   1 2 3 4 5

48. New management programs are introduced all the time in this plant.   1 2 3 4 5

49. In this plant, financial rewards are tied directly to performance.   1 2 3 4 5

50. Department managers at this plant are given authority to run their department as they see fit.   1 2 3 4 5

51. The working environment at this plant changes constantly.   1 2 3 4 5

52. The threat of layoffs of management employees is high.   1 2 3 4 5

53. Cost reduction is the most important objective in this plant.   1 2 3 4 5

54. I am proud to work for this company.   1 2 3 4 5

55. This plant's products are frequently modified by engineering changes.   1 2 3 4 5

56. This plant has had major cutbacks and layoffs in recent years.   1 2 3 4 5

VI. MANAGERIAL WORK ENVIRONMENT

The following questions concern the group of departmental managers, including yourself, who form this plant's management team.

1. This plant's management team has a clear understanding of its work objectives.   1 2 3 4 5

2. When there is disagreement among members of this plant's management team we try to find a compromise.   1 2 3 4 5

3. I would describe this management team as democratic. Managers have an equal say in decisions.   1 2 3 4 5

4. As a member of this plant's management team, I feel that I am really a part of the group.   1 2 3 4 5

5. There are differences of opinion among members of this plant's management team.   1 2 3 4 5

6. Members of management have a clear understanding of what is expected of them.   1 2 3 4 5

7. There is a strong feeling of camaraderie among members of this plant's management team.   1 2 3 4 5

8. The skills and abilities of members of this plant's management team vary widely.   1 2 3 4 5

9. If a disagreement arises among members of this plant's management team the issue is dealt with in an open fashion.   1 2 3 4 5

10. On this plant management team, everyone's opinions are heard.   1 2 3 4 5

Please answer the following questions by circling the appropriate number using the scale below

1	2	3	4	5
Strongly Disagree	Disagree	Neither Agree nor disagree	Agree	Strongly Agree

DO YOU AGREE OR DISAGREE?

11. I look forward to working with the members of this plant's management team each day.　　1　2　3　4　5

12. Disagreements are rare among members of this plant's management team.　　1　2　3　4　5

13. This plant's managers have similar types of work and educational experience.　　1　2　3　4　5

14. Each member of this plant's management team has a clear idea of the team's goals.　　1　2　3　4　5

15. When a disagreement occurs between members of the plant's management team, the plant manager settles the dispute.　　1　2　3　4　5

16. Some members of the management team are afraid to speak up when they disagree with the group's decision.　　1　2　3　4　5

17. Members of this management team respect one another.　　1　2　3　4　5

18. Members of this plant's management team have very different backgrounds.　　1　2　3　4　5

VII. BACKGROUND INFORMATION

A. Education and Training

1. Please place an 'X' beside the highest level of formal education that you attained:

   High school diploma or equivalency exam　　＿＿＿＿＿
   Associates degree (2 years of college training)　＿＿＿＿＿
   Bachelors degree (4 years of college training)　＿＿＿＿＿　　Field　＿＿＿＿＿＿＿＿
   Masters degree　　＿＿＿＿＿　　Field　＿＿＿＿＿＿＿＿
   Other　　＿＿＿＿＿　　Field　＿＿＿＿＿＿＿＿

2. Please place an 'X' beside the types of training that you have received in activity based costing. Then estimate the total hours that each course devoted to the topic of activity-based costing.

Types of Training		ABC hours	
Degree-granting educational programs	＿＿＿	Total ABC class hours:	＿＿＿
Non-degree courses offered by external provider	＿＿＿	Total ABC class hours:	＿＿＿
Non-degree courses offered by the company	＿＿＿	Total ABC class hours:	＿＿＿
On the job training designed to teach about ABC	＿＿＿		
No training in ABC	＿＿＿		

3. Please place an 'X' beside the statement that <u>best</u> reflects your level of knowledge about the <u>general concepts</u> of activity based costing.

   I've never heard of activity based costing　　＿＿＿＿＿
   I've heard of activity based costing, but I don't really know much about it　　＿＿＿＿＿
   I understand the basic concepts of activity based costing　　＿＿＿＿＿
   I know a great deal about activity based costing　　＿＿＿＿＿
   I consider myself an expert in activity based costing　　＿＿＿＿＿

4.   Please place an 'X' beside the statement that <u>best</u> reflects your level of knowledge about the <u>implementation</u> of activity based costing at this plant.

I didn't know that this plant had an activity based costing system   _____
I'm aware that this plant has ABC, but I don't know much about it   _____
I'm aware that this plant has ABC and I have a general understanding of it   _____
I'm aware that this plant has ABC and know a great deal about it   _____
I am an expert in this plant's ABC system   _____

B. Work History

5.   How many years have you worked at this company? (round up to the nearest full year) _____ yrs.

6.   How many years have you worked at this plant? (round up to the nearest full year) _____ yrs.

7.   How many hourly employees are in your department?   _____

8.   How many salaried employees are in your department?   _____

9.   How many of the hourly employees are union members?   _____

10.   How many of the salaried employees are represented by a bargaining unit?   _____

11.   Please provide information about the last two jobs that you have had. Begin with your current job and then provide information about the job that you held before that.

a) Current Job title _____ Department _____

Job Description: _____

Period of employment: FROM: _____ year   TO: _____ year

b) Job title _____ Department _____

Job Description: _____

Company Name (if different): _____

Period of employment: FROM: _____ year   TO: _____ year

178

If there is anything else that you would like to tell us about the plant or the ABC project, please use the space below.

Thank you for your assistance in helping us gather information about ABC implementation at this plant.

REFERENCES

Algina, J., and S. Olejnik. 2000. Determining Sample Size for Accurate Estimation of the Squared Multiple Correlation Coefficient. *Multivariate Behavioral Research* 35(1): 119-137.

Anderson, S. W. 1995. A Framework for Assessing Cost Management System Changes: The Case of Activity Based Costing Implementation at General Motors, 1986-1993. *Journal of Management Accounting Research* (7): 1-51.

Anderson, S. W., and S. M. Young. 1999. The Impact of Contextual and Process Factors. On the Evaluation of Activity Based Costing Systems. *Accounting, Organizations and Society* (24): 525-559.

Anderson, S. W., J. Hesford and S. M. Young. 2001. Factors Influencing the Performance of Activity Based Costing Teams: A Field Study of ABC Model Development in the Automobile Industry. Working Paper, Marshall School of Business, University of Southern California.

Argyris, C., and R. Kaplan. 1994. Implementing New Knowledge: The Case of activity Based Costing." *Accounting Horizons* (September): 83-105.

Armstrong, D. 1990a. How Rockwell Launched its EIS. *Datamation* 36 (March 10): 69-72.

Armstrong, D. 1990b. The People Factor in EIS Success. *Datamation* 36 (April 1): 78-79

Bagozzi, R. P., and T. F. Heatherton. 1994 A General Approach to Representing Multifaceted Personality Constructs: Application to State and Self-Esteem. *Structural Equation Modeling* 1(1): 35-67.

Bagozzi, R. P., and Y. Yi. 1988 On the Evaluation of Structural Equation Models. *Journal of the Academy of Marketing Science* 16(1): 74-94.

Bakos, J. Y. and C. F. Kemerer 1992. Recent Applications of Economic Theory in Information Technology Research. *Decision Support Systems* 8 (5): 365-86.

Barclay, D., C. Higgins and R. Thompson. 1995. The Partial Least Squares (PLS) Approach to Causal Modeling. Personal Computer Adoption and Use as an Illustration. *Technology Studies*: 285-324.

Beaujon, G. J., and V. R. Singhal. 1990. Understanding the Activity Costs in and Activity-based Cost System. *Journal of Cost Management* (Spring): 51-72.

Bettenhausen, K. L. 1991. Five Years of Teams Research: What We Have Learned and What Needs to be Addressed. *Journal of Management* (17): 345-381.

Bostrom, R. P., and J. S. Heinan. 1977. MIS Problems and Failures: A Socio-Technical Perspective. *MIS Quarterly*: 11-28.

Box, G. E. P., W. G. Hunter and J. S. Hunter. 1978. *Statistics for Experimenters*. New York: John Wiley and Sons.

Brausch, J. M. 1992. Selling ABC. *Management Accounting* (February): 42-46.

180

Brynjolfsson, E. 1993. The Productivity Paradox of Information Technology. *Communications of the ACM*. 36 (12): 66-77.

Brynjolfsson, E. and S. Yang. 1996. Information Technology and Productivity: A Review of the Literature. *Advances in Computers*. 43: 179-214.

Chin, W.W., and P. R. Newsted. 1999. Structural Equation Modeling Analysis with Small Samples Using Partial Least Squares. In R.H. Hoyle (Ed.), *Statistical strategies for Small Sample Research*. Thousand Oaks, CA: Sage Publications, Inc.: 307-341.

Cohen, S. 1993. New Approaches to Teams and Teamwork. In J. Galbraith and E. E. Lawler III. *Organizing for the Future*. San Francisco: Jossey Bass Publishers: 194-226.

Cohen, S. G., and D. E. Bailey. 1997. What Makes Teams Work: Group Effectiveness Research from the Shop Floor to the Executive Suite. *Journal of Management* (23): 239-290.

Cooper, R. 1988. The Rise of Activity Based Costing - Part One: What is an Activity-Based Cost System? *Journal of Cost Management* (Summer): 45-54.

Cooper, R., 1990. Implementing an Activity-based Cost System. *Journal of Cost Management* (Spring): 33-42.

Cooper, R., and R. S. Kaplan. 1988. Measure Costs Right: Make the right decisions. *Harvard Business Review* (September-October): 96-105.

Cooper, R., and R. S. Kaplan. 1991. *The Design of Cost Management Systems – Text, Cases and Readings*. Englewood Cliffs, N. J.: Prentice Hall.

Cooper, R., R. S. Kaplan, R. S., Maisel, L. S., Morrissey, E., and R. E. Oehm. 1992. *Implementing Activity-Based Cost Management: Moving From Analysis to Action*. (Montvale, N. J.: Institute of Management Accountants).

Cooper, R., and P. B. B. Turney. 1990. Internally Focused Activity-Based Cost Systems. In Robert S. Kaplan (ed.), *Measures for Manufacturing Excellence*. Boston, MA: Harvard Business School Press.: 291-305.

Cooper, R., and R. W. Zmud. 1990. Information Technology Implementation Research: A Technological Diffusion Approach. *Management Science* 36 (20): 123-139.

Datar, S. M., and M. Gupta. 1994. Aggregation, Specification and Measurement Errors in Product Costing. *The Accounting Review* (69): 567-591.

Davis, F. D. 1989. Perceived Usefulness, Perceived Ease of Use, and User Acceptance of Information technology." *MIS Quarterly* 13(3): 319-340.

Davis, F. D., R. P. Bagozzi, and P. R. Warshaw. 1989. User Acceptance of Computer Technology: A Comparison of Two Theoretical Models." *Management Science* 23(8): 982-1003.

DeLone, W. H., and E. R. McLean. 1992. Information Systems Success: The Quest for the Dependent Variable. *Information Systems Research* (3): 60-95.

Drake, A., S. Haka and S. Ravenscroft. 1999. Cost System and Incentive Structure Effects on Innovation, Efficiency and Profitability in Teams. *The Accounting Review* (74): 323-346.

Drumheller, H. K., Jr. 1993. Making Activity-Based Costing Practical. *Journal of Cost Management* (Summer): 21-27.

Efron, B., and R. J. Tibshirani. 1993. *An Introduction to the Bootstrap.* New York: Chapman & Hall.

Eiler, R. G., and J. P. Campi. 1990. Implementing Activity-Based Costing at a Process Company." *Journal of Cost Management* (Spring): 43-50.

Fireworker, R. W., and W. Zirkel. 1990. Designing and EIS in a Multi-divisional Environment. *Journal of Systems Management* (February): 25-31

Fisher, R. P., and R. E. Geiselman. 1992. *Memory-Enhancing Techniques for Investigative Interviewing.* Springfield, IL: Charles C. Thomas Publisher.

Fornell, C., and F. L. Bookstein. (1982). A Comparative Analysis of Two Structural Equation Models: LISREL and PLS Applied to Market Data. In C. Fornell (Ed.), *A Second Generation of Multivariate Analysis.* (289-324). New York: Praeger Publishers.

Foster, George, and M. Gupta. 1990. Activity Accounting: An Electronics Industry Implementation." In R. S Kaplan (ed.), *Measures for Manufacturing Excellence*: 291-305. Boston, MA: Harvard Business School Press.

Foster, George, and Dan W. Swenson. 1997. Measuring the Success of Activity-Based Cost Management and its Determinants. *Journal of Management Accounting Research* (9): 109-142.

Franz, C. R., and D. Robey. 1984. An Investigation of User-Led System Design: Rational and Political Perspectives. *Communications of the ACM* 27 (12): 1202-1209.

Galbraith, J., and E. E. Lawler III. 1993. *Organizing for the Future.* San Francisco, CA.: Jossey-Bass.

Gladstein, D.L. 1984. Teams in Context: A Model of Task Team Effectiveness. *Administrative Science Quarterly* 29 (December): 499-517.

Ginzberg. M. J. 1981. Early Diagnosis of MIS Failure: Promising Results and Unanswered Questions. *Management Science* (27): 459-478.

Goodman, P. S., E. Ravlin, and M. Schminke. 1987. Understanding Teams in Organizations. *Research in Organizational Behavior.* JAI press: 121-173.

Gosselin, M. 1997. The Effects of Strategy and Organizational Structure on the Adoption and Implementation of ABC. *Accounting, Organizations and Society* (22): 105-122.

Guzzo, R. A., and G. P. Shea. 1992. Team Performance and Interteam Relations in Organizations. In *Handbook of Industrial and Organ-izational Psychology*, 2nd ed., (edited by M. D. Dunnette and L. M. Hough). Palo Alto, CA: Consulting Psychologists Press: 269-313.

182

Hackman, J. R. 1987. The Design of Work Teams. *Handbook of Organ-izational Behavior*: 315-342.

Hackman, J. R., and G. R. Oldham. 1976. Motivation Through the Design of Work: Test of a Theory. *Organizational Behavior and Human Performance*: 250-279.

Hackman, J. R., and G. R. Oldham. 1980. *Work Redesign*. Reading, Mass.: Addison Wesley Publishing Company.

Haedicke, J., and D. Feil. 1991. In a DoD Environment: Hughes Aircraft sets the Standard for ABC. *Management Accounting* (February): 29-33.

Harris, R. J. (1975). *A Primer of Multivariate Statistics*. New York: Academic.

Hallam, G., and D. Campbell. 1994. *Test Manual for the Campbell-Hallam Team Development Survey*. Minnetonka, Minnesota: NCS Assessments.

Hulland, J. 1998. Use of Partial Least Squares in Strategic Management Research. *Comportamento Organizacional E. Ges* (4): 181-202.

Ives, B., and M. H. Olson. 1984. User Involvement and MIS Success: A Review of Research. *Management Science*: 586-603.

James, L. R., R. G. Demaree and G. Wolf. 1984. Estimating Within-Group Interrater Reliability With and Without Response Bias. *Journal of Applied Psychology* (69): 85-98.

Jaworski, B., and S. M. Young. 1992. Dysfunctional Behavior and Management Control: An Empirical Study of Marketing Managers. *Accounting, Organizations and Society* (17): 17-35.

Jones, Lou F. 1991. Product Costing at Caterpillar." *Management Accounting*, (February): 34-42

Kanter, R. M., B. A. Stein and T. D. Jick. 1992. *The Challenge of Organizational Change*. NewYork, NY: Free Press.

Kaplan, Robert S. 1990. The Four-Stage Model of Cost System Design. *Management Accounting* (February): 22-26.

Kaplan, R. S., and R. Cooper. 1998. *Cost and Effect*. Boston, MA: Harvard Business School Press.

Katzenbach, J. R., and D. K. Smith. 1995. *The Wisdom of Teams*. Boston, MA: Harvard Business School Press.

Kolodny, H., and M. Kiggundu. 1980. Towards the Development of a Socio-Technical Systems Model in Woodland Mechanical Harvesting. *Human Relations*: 623-645.

Kleinsorge, I. K., and R. D. Tanner. 1991. Activity-Based Costing: Eight Questions to Answer Before You Implement. *Journal of Cost Management* (Fall): 84-88.

Krumwiede, K. R. 1998. The Implementation Stages of Activity-based Costing and the Impact of Contextual and Organizational Factors. *Journal of Management Accounting Research* (10): 239-277.

Kwon, T. H., and R. W. Zmud. 1987. Unifying the Fragmented Models of Information Systems Implementation. In R. J. Boland and R. Hirscheim (eds.), *Critical Issues in Information Systems Research*. New York: John Wiley.

Lawler, E. E. III., S. A Mohrman, and G. E. Ledford, Jr. 1995. *Creating High Performance Organizations*. San Francisco, Jossey-Bass.

Leonard-Barton, D., and W. Kraus. 1985. Implementing New Technology. *Harvard Business Review* (November-December): 102-110.

Lewin, K. 1943. Psychology and the Process of Team Living. *Journal of Social Psychology*: 113-31.

Lindquist, K., and J. Mauriel. 1989. Depth and Breadth in Innovation Implementation: The Case of School-based Management. In Andrew H. Van de Ven, H. Angle and Marshall Scott Poole (eds.), *Research on the Management of Innovation: The Minnesota Studies*: 561-82. New York: Ballinger/ Harper and Row.

Markus, M. L. 1983. Power, Politics, and MIS Implementation. *Commu-nications of the ACM* (26): 430-444.

Markus, M. L. 1984. *Systems in Organizations*. Marshfield, MA: Pitman Publishing Company.

Marcus, A, and M. Weber. 1989. Externally Induced Innovation. In Andrew H. Van de Ven, H. Angle and Marshall Scott Poole (eds.), *Research on the Management of Innovation: The Minnesota Studies*: 537-60. New York: Ballinger/ Harper and Row.

McGowan, A. S, and T. P. Klammer. 1997. Satisfaction with Activity-Based Cost Management Implementation. *Journal of Management Accounting Research* (9): 217-237.

McLennan, R. 1989. *Managing Organizational Change*. Englewood Cliffs, NJ: Prentice-Hall.

Mohrman, S., S. Cohen, and M. Mohrman, Jr. 1995. *Designing Team-Based Organizations*. San Francisco, CA.: Jossey-Bass.

Morton, M. S. S., Ed. 1991. *The Corporation of the 1990s: Information Technology and Organizational Transformation*. New York, NY: Oxford University Press.

Mumford, E. 1983. Successful Systems Design. In *New Office Technology: Human and Organizational Aspects*, edited by H. Otway and M. Peltu, 68-85. Norwood, NJ: Ablex.

Ness, J. A., and T. G. Cucuzza. 1995. Tapping the Full Potential of ABC. *Harvard Business Review* (95): 130-138.

Noreen, E. and N. Soderstrom. 1994. Are Overhead Costs Strictly Proportional to Activity? *Journal of Accounting and Economics* (17): 255-278.

Nunnally, J. C. 1978. *Pyschometric Theory*. 2nd Ed. New York: McGraw-Hill.

Player, S. and D. Keys, 1995. *Activity Based Management: Lessons from the ABM Battlefield.* New York: MasterMedia Limited.

Pedhazur, E. J., and L. P. Schmelkin. 1991. *Measurement, Design, and Analysis.* Hillsdale, NJ: Lawrence Erlbaum Associates, Publishers.

Porter, M. E. 1980. *Competitive Strategy.* New York: Free Press.

Prein, H. C. M. 1984. A Contingency Approach to Conflict Management. *Group and Organizations Studies* 9: 81-102.

Richards, P. R. 1987. Managing Costs Strategically. *Journal of Cost Management* (Summer): 11-20.

Robey, D. 1981. Computer Information Systems and Organization Structure. *Communications of the ACM* 24(10): 679-687.

Robinson, J. P., P. R. Shaver, and L. S. Wrightsman. 1991. *Measures of Personality and Social Psychological Attitudes.* New York: Harcourt Brace Jovanovich, Publishers.

Rogers, Everett M.1983. *Diffusion of Innovations,* 3rd Ed. New York: The Free Press.

Rousseau, D. M. 1985. Issues of Level in Organizational research: Multi-level and cross-level perspectives. *Research in Organizational Behavior* (7): 1-37.

Safizadeh, M. H. 1991. The Case of Workgroups in Manufacturing Operations. *California Management Review* 33 61-82.

Seashore, S. E., E. E. Lawler III, P. H. Mirvis, and C. Cammann. 1983. *Assessing Organizational Change.* New York: John Wiley and Sons.

Seidler, J. 1974. On Using Informants: A Technique for Collecting Quantitative Data and Controlling Measurement Error in Organization Analysis. *American Sociological Review* (39): 816-833.

Shields, M. D. 1997. Research in Management Accounting by North Americans in the 1990s. *Journal of Management Accounting Research* (9): 3-62.

Shields, M. D., and S. M. Young. 1989. A Behavioral Model for Implementing Cost Management Systems. *Journal of Cost Management* (Winter): 17-27.

Shields, Michael D. 1995. An Empirical Analysis of Firms' Implementation Experiences with Activity-Based Costing. *Journal of Management Accounting Research* (Fall): 1-28.

Shrout, P. E., and J. L. Fleiss. 1979. Intraclass Correlations: Uses in Assessing Rater Reliability. *Psychological Bulletin* (2): 420-428.

Spreitzer, G. M. 1995. Psychological Empowerment in the Workplace: Dimensions, Measurement, and Validation. *Academy of Management Journal* (38): 1442-1465.

Stine, R. 1989. An Introduction to Bootstrapping Methods: Examples and Ideas. *Sociological Methods and Research* (18): 243-291.

Stokes, C. R., and K. W. Lawrimore. 1989. Selling a New Cost System. *Journal of Cost Management* (Fall): 29-34.

Swenson, D. W. 1995. The Benefits of Activity-Based Cost Management to the Manufacturing Industry. *Journal of Management Accounting Research* (7): 167-180.

Tabachnick, B. G., and L. S. Fidell. 1989. *Using Multivariate Statistics*. 2nd ed. Cambridge, MA: Harper & Row.

Thomas, K. W. 1976. Conflict and Conflict Management. In M. D. Dunnette (Ed.), *Handbook of Industrial and Organizational Psychology*, Chicago: Rand McNally, 889-935.

Turney, P. 1992. Common Cents – The ABC Performance Breakthrough. Hillsboro, OR: Cost Technology.

Van de Ven, Andrew H. 1993. Managing the Process of Organizational Innovation. In George P. Huber and W. H. Glick (eds.), *Organizational Change and Redesign*. New York: Oxford University Press.

Van de Ven, A. H., and D. L. Ferry. 1980. *Measuring and Assessing Organizations*. New York: John Wiley and Sons.

Wageman, R. 1995. Interdependence and Team Effectiveness. *Administrative Science Quarterly* (40): 145-180.

Young, S. M. 1997. Field Research Methods in Management Accounting. *Accounting Horizons* (March, 1999): 76-84.

Young, S. M. 1997. Implementing Management Innovations Successfully: Some Principles for Lasting Change. *Journal of Cost Management* (Spring): 16-20.

Young, S. M., J. Fisher and T. Lindquist. 1993. The Effects of Varying Intergroup Competition and Intragroup Cooperation on Slack and Output in a Manufacturing Setting. *The Accounting Review* (July): 466-48d.

Young, S. M., and Selto, F. 1993. Explaining Cross-sectional Workgroup Performance Differences in a JIT facility: A Critical Appraisal of a Field-Based Study. *Journal of Management Accounting Research* (5): 300-326.

Zaltman, G., R. Duncan, R. 1977. *Strategies for Planned Change*. New York: John Wiley and Sons, Inc.

Zuboff, S. 1988. *In the Age of the Smart Machine: The Future of Work and Power*. New York, NY: Basic Books.

INDEX

DATE DUE